Walking
when you'd rather fly

meditations on faith after the fall

Amy Clemens

This book is dedicated to my daughters, beautiful souls;
yet perhaps the two least likely to understand its
contents now. I am the one who got to choose their names
the first time, names meaning *beloved* and *heroine*, and
they are that to me. It is my prayer that the God who loves
them even more than I will heal their hearts from
the pain they experienced in childhood and give them the
capacity someday, to not only understand, but overcome, to
find nourishment from a secret source
and that incredible new name.

*To the one who is victorious, I will give some of the hidden
manna. I will also give that person a white stone with a new
name written on it, known only to the one who receives it.*
Revelation 2:17 NIV

TABLE OF CONTENTS

Like a wave that hasn't crested
A half-done work of art
A banquet interrupted
Or passion with no heart
Like a dancer in mid-air
Or a song that has no start
I'm half blind at this shoreline
Watching waters that won't part, oh

Mine is an unfinished life
With races to run
And pages to write
If I'm walking by faith
And not just by sight
Then mine is an unfinished life

January 2008

PREFACE

I've had dreams of flying since I was a little girl. Not in an airplane, mind you, but with my body, like a bird, free on the breeze. Occasionally in my dreams, a jet pack strapped to my back gave lift, but more often, it was just me, arms outstretched, gently hovering over the earth, reveling in stillness and vastness, with a weightless body and pain-free spirit. There was never any fear attached to these dreams, never any crashes or near misses. The heavens were mine it would seem, and so I just simply and naturally flew. What else would I do?

As I look back, I think these were dreams about freedom and what I thought it looked and felt like. Internally, freedom is something I've rarely felt but always longed for, and that truth has seriously complicated my journey as a Christian. When the dreams were over and I woke up, I still wanted to fly but, like a pilot grounded for some breach of rules, it would seem these feet were made for walking.

From an early age, I knew that Christians had been set free, because Mom, the pastor, and my Sunday school teacher raved about it. It was obviously a good thing, but try as I might, I couldn't capture that feeling. In fact, the older I got, the less free I felt, trading in childhood dreams for a life in which I felt hemmed in and judged and "not good enough" no matter how I tried. As you read on, you'll understand more about why I struggled so, but for now, let's just say that the guilt of not getting "freedom in Christ" became like one of those weights that dangles at the bottom of a bunch of balloons, grounding them for the enjoyment of others. Not ironically, the grounded me became good at making others happy, voted most humorous of my senior class, and Miss Congeniality twice in the county beauty pageant. I was driven to succeed, driven to "fly high" by the achievement and possibility thinkers of the 70s and 80s, but it was falling, not flying, that seemed to most define me. Christianity became one more thing I could never get quite right. I used to wonder aloud, "How can I be a perfectionist if I never get anything right?" Now, I laugh at the irony of that statement, because only a perfectionist would say such a thing!

In my late fifties and many falls later, I still wouldn't say I fly through life, but I've learned to walk, and I keep getting up and walking on, despite bumps, bruises, hospitalizations, sporadic skinned knees, several broken hearts, and sometimes earth-bound spirits. Miraculously, I've tasted the freedom of flying as I've allowed Jesus to come beside me and rescue me in the midst of long, hard falls; to fly with me to a safe place and there set me on my feet again. Someday I hope I can look back on my decision to just keep walking as a good one. A steady commitment to trust God despite everything that happened, everything that went wrong, everything that didn't make sense – because it's not the life of perfection that pleases God, it's the life of faith. We're all living unfinished lives. There's hope as long as there's ink in the pen.

This book is my way of encouraging you in the life of faith too. We all have a place in the *Big Story* God is telling. Understanding the big picture, the context for that story, helped me find my own place in it. Perhaps things have gone swimmingly for you, and if so, I'm grateful, and these words may not mean much. On the other hand, if you believe in God but are confused about how difficult life is, maybe you'll find something here that helps you fly someday. Or, in the meantime at least, helps you get up, again and again, to walk when you'd rather fly.

PART 1: THE BIG PICTURE
What on Earth is Going On?

Do you have a word for me now?
God of my past and my future, somehow
Can you call something new out of long-buried seed
Out of water and dirt and me?

Break up this soil where it's just rocks and weeds
Call fruitfulness from this ground drenched with tears
I wait for your voice, offer my offering –
Use this water and dirt and me.

Could Genesis come out of chaos again?
Would you call light from darkness and blue sky from rain?
Oh a garden could grow if you speak just a word
Into water and dirt and me

July 2017

Chapter 1
Water, Dirt and Us

As a father has compassion on his children,
so the Lord has compassion on those who fear him;
for he knows how we are formed,
he remembers that we are dust.
Psalm 103:13-14 NIV

Did you ever stop to think that if the Bible is really true, we are smack in the middle of the most incredible experiment of all time? A sweeping experiment of romance that traverses panoramic heights and hidden valleys, great deserts, and impossible seas. A lover looking for his beloved, roaming vast reaches of time and geography to find her.

The *fait accompli* is problematic, however – for both lover and the beloved he pursues.

He created her, this companion he pursues, from his rich imagination. A creature that would be in his own likeness; not him, but made like him with capacities to rule and create and bring life. Capacity for wholeness and relationship and love. Fire for justice and longing for mercy. A knowledge that it wasn't good to be alone and a drive toward fulfilling relationship.

Then, unlike his other creations which were made with his words, he got down into creation and got dirty, shaping her with his own hands out of his other creation. He got up close and personal, putting his mouth on hers and breathing life into this heart he would pursue.

Enter the experiment.

Knowing that love requires freedom, he gave the new life free reign to choose as she would. He had given her greatness. Made her capable. More intelligent than anything else he had created. But would she choose to love her Creator, the one who knew her inside out and loved her so much he gave her *freedom above all else*, or would she be wooed away by other lovers, perhaps because they flattered her with attention, lavished her with gifts, or just were easier in a whole host of ways than loving someone so…well, perfect. In her relationship to Creator, perhaps she would feel her subordination rather than his love. Her free will, the very way she had been created, might urge her to know and do and be more, rather than know and love him and what he had done. Even if those lovers were lesser lovers and would replace the freedom he had given her with bondage.

We are she.

We are the experiment, and from the opening lines of Scripture to its last, our Creator, with everything to lose and little to gain, made a bet that his great love would win in the end. I say "little to gain" because God could have chosen to exist as he already was, and had been, and would be eternally. There was nothing wrong in his 'world.' God was perfect in God's self. He had love, companionship, unity, power, and eternity at his command. God was unconquerable. So why take this crazy risk? What did he stand to gain…and what did he stand to lose?

We are God's risk. He believes true *agape* love will overwhelm the virtues and vices of others who call to us; will captivate and fulfill us. So, yeah, we may feel a little toyed-with somehow, being involved in an experiment we didn't have any say in. But before we get too carried away with our indignation, let's consider who had the most to lose. We got life, with all its triumph and tragedy. But God? After it became obvious, almost right away, that we *would indeed* choose to give our affection to liars, peddling promises of gain and lifting lofty visions of what we were missing, God spent the rest of the experiment basically mopping up from the risk he had taken and trying to right his world again.

The experiment all went awry, but here's the startling truth: Being God, God was prepared for this possibility. And still, he made the decision to pour self-giving love out on creation. Unlike lesser lovers, he keeps his promises and continues to pursue us. To show us compassion and remember we are made of dust. To woo us back. To whisper love to us in the darkest moments of our lives.

> *Therefore I am now going to allure her; I will lead her into the wilderness and speak tenderly to her. There I will give her back her vineyards, and will make the Valley of Achor a door of hope. There she will respond as in the days of her youth, as in the day she came up out of Egypt.* (Hosea 2:14-15 NIV)

Have you ever felt wooed into a wilderness? A desert, where there was nothing but burning sun and sand? So weakened by the elements all you could do was sit and try to make sense of the view, distorted as it was by heat waves. At night you shivered, so cold you wished for the heat; in the day you shrank to the shadow of even a spindly cactus, wishing for the night.

The *Valley of Achor* means the valley of trouble – and that was my home until I was in my 40s. You will read that story further on, but for now, trust me when I say that being led into the wilderness doesn't sound like love. But when you're truly alone, in pain, empty as a rain barrel in a drought, sitting in a desert where your biggest distractions are hunger, thirst, and the occasional viper, you listen differently when *that voice* speaks tenderly to you.

Sometimes we get so caught up in our own stories of love and loss and betrayal we forget there even *is* a bigger story. We forget, when we rub our head in anguish over our latest defeat or pace the floors at night, that our slice of life is just one blip on the timeline God sees. It's part of his holy experiment – will we love him or the idols we have made? We forget the Big Story: *It's all God's*. He made it all (Genesis 1), he owns it all (Psalm 24:1), he loves it all (John 3:16), and he sacrificed himself for it all (Romans 5:17).

And why does his love continue to chase us down, against all odds? *Because he named us "Bride."* The longer you sit with that name, the more fascinating it becomes, and the more you begin to see that the whole story of God is telling the same tale – a lover pursuing the one he wants to unite with forever. *Us.* This is part of why marriage is such a sacred bond. It is bound deeply into the center of God's longings. It is not a sham, a bond of convenience, or a place to hide from our fears. It is not a thing we do just because it seems logical. The stakes are too big, and I know that truth by the scars on my own heart. Marriage is a place to experience naked vulnerability. To be known, to let the walls down and let your truest self be seen, to be treasured and treasure another despite what is known and seen. A place where passion can provoke the fiercest jealousy known, and betrayal melt the soul. A place where husband

and wife reclothe each other's vulnerabilities with kindness, strength, and appropriate armor for the warfare that takes place beyond the sacred covenant.

Scripture says, "God is love," and holds that true, self-giving love is the most powerful force known. But we continue to invest in our running, our pandering, our self-pleasing, our little stories. We continue to explore the height and depth and breadth of our own resources rather than the height and depth and breadth of God's. We break ourselves and wreck our world with selfishness and violence, pursuing the desires of the flesh and the desires of the eyes and pride of life (1 John 2:16).

I think of it as *living into the fall*, rather than learning from it. We act as if humans are cursed by God in the fall, somehow locked into a battle for control and domination. No! For whatever reasons (and wouldn't it be wonderful to talk with God about this), the curse God pronounced fell on the earth we were created from instead of us, and it fell on the one who had wooed us with lies (Genesis 3:14-19).

The *results* of those curses are felt deeply, daily: weeds (both relationally and literally), frustration and pain, sin and suffering, and ultimately the death assured if the fruit of the knowledge of good and evil was even touched (Genesis 3:3). But we aren't locked into them with no escape. In fact, the Christian life is all about breaking free from the bondage we experience, sometimes due to others' sin, sometimes due to our own.

Our enemy is cursed, not us. The ground is cursed and longs for its release (Romans 8:21), when it *will join us* in the freedom from death and decay we already enjoy. We are not cursed; we are loved beyond all reason!

> *Against its will, all creation was subjected to God's curse. But with eager hope, the creation looks forward to the day when it will join God's children in glorious freedom from death and decay. For we know that all creation has been groaning as in the*

pains of childbirth right up to the present time. And we believers also groan, even though we have the Holy Spirit within us as a foretaste of future glory, for we long for our bodies to be released from sin and suffering (Romans 8:20-23 NLT).

In the tension between freedom from groaning and living on planet earth, the God of heaven and earth pursues, ready to pour his self-giving love on us. He waits for us to be broken by our self-efforts at creating life and finding substitutes for love. He longs for our return to him, confident in the knowledge that love does not fail (1 Corinthians 13:8); it rescues and redeems (Deuteronomy 7:8) and it covers a multitude of sin (1 Peter 4:8) so well that it can't be found again (Psalm 103:12).

He knows that his experiment works if we will only turn toward his love.

From one man he created all the nations throughout the whole earth. He decided beforehand when they should rise and fall, and he determined their boundaries. His purpose was for the nations to seek after God and perhaps feel their way toward him and find him—though he is not far from any one of us. (Acts 17:26-27 NLT)

From the wreckage of childhood abuse and its subsequent relational, vocational and spiritual pain, I've been feeling my way toward God, seeking one who could redeem my story. When I turned toward him, he did his creative best, making "a Genesis week from the chaos of my life," as Eugene Peterson's *Message* puts it so eloquently. He took water, dirt, and me, and made something grow out of a long-buried seed. It's still not fully grown, but it's taking shape and I have complete confidence that he will bring it to a good completion (Philippians 1:6).

If you're in need of a genesis, I pray you might let the God who made and loves you do his fine work in your story too.

God, make a fresh start in me, shape a Genesis week from the chaos of my life.
Psalm 51:10 MSG

Chapter 1: Water, Dirt & Us
QUESTIONS FOR REFLECTION

Question: Being wired with the freedom to choose has both up and down sides: Name the two of each that are most significant in your story:

Question: How has someone else's freedom to choose hurt you? How has your own freedom to choose hurt you? Others? God?

Question: How does the idea of God risking everything for the experiment of human freedom sit with you? If you could pretend to be God for a moment, what would you do to win the hearts and minds of humans without messing with free will?

Question: How does what you've believed about the curse differ from Scripture's reading that the curse falls on the earth and the one who tempts with lies?

Action: If it's true that God is a lover pursuing his beloved across all of time and space, he is also pursuing you through pain, dysfunction, things that have gone wrong – even ways you've been hurt or hurt others. Using this lens, pretend you are God the Lover for a bit and write a letter to yourself. What would God the Lover say? How have you been pursued by kindness and love?

Bull's-eye, the arrow hit its perfect mark
Shot to pierce through the deepest part of you
So it left its fiery trail
And a hole right through your heart
Yet nothing in the world could stop the flow
That started when the arrow hit its mark

July 2006

Chapter 2
Target Practice

"All right, you may test him," the Lord said to Satan. "Do whatever you want with everything he possesses, but don't harm him physically."
So Satan left the Lord's presence.
Job 1:12 NLT

Don't you feel a little chill when you read Job? If you need further evidence that there is an experiment going on, this story furnishes it. Satan leaves the courtroom described in the previous six verses, goes out and kills Job's children, ruins his fortunes, shreds his reputation as a righteous soul, then ultimately, snatches his health by the end of the second chapter.

This is not just some random story; it is very purposefully included in Scripture, introducing the two largest actors in the Big Story of God: God, and God's adversary. Most scholars believe Job is the oldest book of the Bible, its story predating the law and prophets, teaching the ancient Hebrews and all readers throughout time who this God of gods is, even before covenant and law. Spelling out an ancient battle between good and evil.

Although it's unlike any other book of the Bible, it's far from the only text that deals with suffering, pain, and the voice of the accuser. That voice, and his many names, appear in stories from the Garden of Eden in Genesis 3, to the final pages of Revelation.

Job doesn't know about the conversation that has taken place between God and Satan concerning his integrity. Satan has spotted a strong heart and asks permission to break it down. Satan tries to *accuse God* with language he knows so well. *Surely you don't believe, God, that Job loves you for you....* He essentially calls God foolish for thinking Job really loves him. But God knows Job's heart and it beats after his own, so God allows the test because he believes Job will not fail to love him or seek to malign his character. In essence, God does not believe himself a fool to *trust* Job!

But poor Job; he does believe himself a fool at points. He wants to die sometimes; he demands to know why. In his deep pain, he argues with God, but he won't turn his back.

For some reason, this story captured me as a little kid. I prayed to be like Job, steady through heartache. Faithfulness, God knew, would be a long journey. It took me four decades to really read the whole story through to its end. To fully take it in and ponder its meaning. To get over my initial recoil at the idea that my life could have anything to do with a war between God and Satan; with the love experiment and the one invested in its failure. To see

that the pat answers of Job's friends, their wrongful
accusations about his integrity, made God angry.

I have lived long enough now that Job's story can be
used as a lens to examine my own.

In the big picture, this ancient narrative of God's
courtroom explains a lot of the chaos we see around us with
evidence you may have dismissed. I know I did. If you say
you trust Jesus and love God, but you have somehow
overlooked Satan, well, Satan has you exactly where Satan
wants you, and trust me, this evil presence doesn't want
you to believe its existence, because the work to be
accomplished is so much more easily done under the radar.

Consider the court in heaven again for a moment:

> *One day the members of the heavenly court came to*
> *present themselves before the Lord, and the*
> *Accuser, Satan, came with them.* (Job 1:6 NLT).

Like a hungry prosecuting attorney, Satan comes to
court prepared to trample on the defense. The accuser's job
is 1) to accuse, and 2) to get us to imitate him. If he can get
us to accuse ourselves, we will practice self-contempt and
not be able to accept grace. If he can get us to accuse
others, we will practice other-centered contempt and not be
able to show mercy. And if he can get us to accuse God,
that's his sweetest bullseye of all, because once you believe
God is not good, the seeds of mistrust, skepticism, and
distance grow until you think God a fable, a creation of
weak-minded people needing a crutch. The Apostle Paul, a
redeemed accuser, says that the more distant from God a
person grows, the less clear his or her thinking gets:

> *Yes, they knew God, but they wouldn't worship him*
> *as God or even give him thanks. And they began to*
> *think up foolish ideas of what God was like. As a*
> *result, their minds became dark and confused.*
> *Claiming to be wise, they instead became utter*
> *fools. And instead of worshiping the glorious, ever-*
> *living God, they worshiped idols made to look like*

mere people and birds and animals and reptiles. So God abandoned them to do whatever shameful things their hearts desired (Romans 1:21-24 NLT).

Sadly, I fell into the category of those who worship mere people. I stopped trusting that God was good or in control, and I stopped trusting myself and who he had made me to be. You'll read more about that in chapters 5-13, but for our purposes here, I'll just say that in a long, slow, deliberate set up, Satan messed with my life enough that I hated myself sometimes. Perceived myself as weak and needy – and wasn't too sure of God either.

By discounting the power of the evil one and his hatred of me, I allowed him to work silently and lethally in my life for years. But, entertaining the idea that Satan roams around like a lion, looking for someone to devour (1 Peter 5:8), helped me gain a perspective I was completely missing. Suddenly, my entire story made more sense to me. Maybe not logically, but spiritually I had an epiphany. I had become target practice for Satan: devoured – partially by my own sin, surely – but partially by the sin of others and the enemy of my soul.

Paul put it like this:

> *For we are not fighting against flesh-and-blood enemies, but against evil rulers and authorities of the unseen world, against mighty powers in this dark world, and against evil spirits in the heavenly places.* (Ephesians 6:12 NLT)

As I look back on almost 60 years, there is no part of me that believes what happened in my first four decades of life was just random happenstance. There was strategy and set up, and that feels a lot like what happened to Job.

Unlike Job, who had a heart so steady he would say, "God might kill me, but I have no other hope. I am going to argue my case with him. (Job 13:15)," I never had the confidence to argue with God – that takes a heart with some wholeness. Giving up was innate to me; fighting was conflict and I typically ran the other way. My redeemed self loves it that Job was whole enough, certain enough in who God had made him and strong enough in his relationship with his Maker, to argue. I would just go down without a fight. My gifts in music and writing have been buried several times in my life and shot down in ways that only the person receiving the arrow understands. I've been told I didn't write well enough, didn't sing well enough, was too old, not beautiful enough, too beautiful, intimidating, not sure enough, not anointed. You get the idea. I took the arrows in, never rebuffing them until God began to build something new in me.

The Scriptural concept of a shield of faith (Ephesians 6:16) means something to me now; the idea that we move forward because our faith deflects the "flaming arrows" of this ancient enemy. I get it now, but as a child, the idea that I was even a target never occurred, and as I became a teenager, I tossed the idea of an evil entity entirely. When things went wrong, I toggled between blaming and shaming myself, or doing the same to God, while I made gods of others, trying to build my self-esteem by pleasing people, being nice, letting others win, and otherwise trying to curry favor.

When I was about 30, I took the Myers-Briggs personality type indicator and came out precisely in the middle – on everything! I thought that was pretty cool until the counselor-interpreter said, "Well, either you're the most incredibly balanced person in the world, or you have absolutely no idea who you are."

For the next decade, I chose to believe the former, then life fell apart and it became clear that I was whatever anyone wanted me to be, a chameleon, just hoping to find love and acceptance. I had no backbone, and no way to understand the arrows that kept coming right at the heart of me. And then, completely broken, I was reminded by some wise teachers about the other character in the Big Story I had forgotten, ignored, minimized, and written out of *my* script.

I was wounded and bleeding, but there was one who knew how to stop the bleeding and heal the damage. He took an arrow to the heart too. His blood flowed and the enemy thought he had won. But in the greatest irony of all time, Satan's short-lived victory became his biggest defeat. As Christian songwriters Matt Maher and Mia Fieldes put it so beautifully, Jesus won over the arrows, "trampling over death by death."

DEALING WITH JESUS

If you believe in Jesus, and trust he lived and spoke truth, you will be forced to reckon with evil in the form of the evil one because he did. To do otherwise would be naïve. If you believe that people act in evil ways, and that evil hides in structures and institutions, but don't believe there in an evil identity behind what you see around and within, there is a disconnect in your theology.

I know that sounds harsh; it's meant to be jarring. To jog you out of a place where *The Liar* has you believing some lies. Like he doesn't exist, or it's childish to give him credence, or you will look the fool if you acknowledge his existence. If you keep him as an illusion only needed for weaker people, you get to consider yourself strong, and that's where evil wants you.

In our Western context, the belief that evil seeks human life has been largely ignored; Satan has become a silly costume to wear at Halloween; "The devil made me do it," a catch phrase for blame shifting when we don't want to take responsibility for our own sin. Such nonsense trivializes the enemy of our souls and leaves the door wide open to his covert operations.

A quick review of the gospels will show that Jesus never forgot the presence of evil, and attributed temptation, illness, suicidal tendencies, disruption of God's good work, and demon possession to the one he called "the prince of this world (John 12:31)." Even that title should give us a shiver. The first act of his three years of ministry was 40 days of fasting that ended in a detailed conversation with the person of Satan (Matthew 4, Mark 1, Luke 4). That's pretty powerful evidence if you trust Jesus, yet our culture turns the idea of a supernatural force of wickedness into mockery.

But before I give you my rationale for Evil with a capital "E," let's talk about why brilliant theologians, dedicated scientists, and creative geniuses might not tolerate talk of a supernatural evil being. Here's the thing: If you believe in the capacity of the human or the machine (or some combination of the two) to transcend war, poverty, abuse, racism, pollution, illness, even death – to usher in some brand of utopia – you have a vested interest in believing that war, poverty, abuse, racism, pollution, illness and even death have antidotes, you just need to get the formula right and acquire enough power to use it.

My point is *not* that it is wrong to decry or work to resolve these issues (although some will surely claim that), as there are obviously many, many things wrong in our world that require immense energy, intelligence, and compassion. I'm not trying to spiritualize away our biggest problems; I'm trying to make the point that taking the idea of an evil being off the table is likely about us. *Our* desire for control and confidence that our efforts and thoughts make the difference between good and bad, *our* wager that we have enough power to keep ourselves safe. Ironically, it's also the reason a lot of people don't believe in God. To believe in God, or Satan, chips away at our individualism, our prized independence, our sense that we are big and powerful and sophisticated and unstoppable and can change the outcomes. A worldly faith believes that, if we just work hard enough and do the right things, good will result. To believe otherwise is to fall into despair, and that happens to plenty of people too.

I'd like to suggest another view.

God is bigger than our individualism or our collective greatness. And, surprisingly, God's own plans may not line up with ours for how we spend our years on earth. To buy into the idea that God is a Lover seeking his beloved, means we step into the role of responder rather than activist. That's not okay with people who protect the core of who they are with power, anger, success, pride, or even self-contempt. To respond to God is to give God some of your treasured power. To begin listening for what God has said (and is saying), is yielding to God the right to make calls you've been making for yourself. It can hurt your pride, your control, your sense of judgment and mastery. But if you take that step, and move toward the God revealed in Scripture, it's only a few verses before you encounter, and must deal with, *the evil one*.

But let's don't look at the whole of Scripture and a complete theology of evil. That's bigger than this book. Let's just look at what Jesus said. Using the *English Standard Version* of Scripture, I found love mentioned 42 times in Jesus' ministry (across all gospels, so likely actually fewer times because gospel writers often reuse the same story or teaching). The words "money," "mammon," or "riches," by contrast, appeared only 24 times across the four gospels. But during his three-year public ministry, Jesus talks about evil as an entity and hell as an actual location 87 times across all four gospels: in Matthew 32 times, Mark 15 times, Luke 25 times, and John 15 times.

He speaks of the reality of hell as a destination using four names (hell, hell of fire, unquenchable fire, and eternal fire) in 15 different verses. He talks of demons and demon possession 27 times using four different names (demons, evil spirits, devil's angels, and unclean spirits).

He gives Satan 10 different names (evil, the evil one, Satan, devil, thief, prince of this world, ruler of this world, liar, father of lies, and murderer), talking about the reality of Satan an astonishing 45 times, including this thoroughgoing diatribe to the religious elite of his day:

> *You are the children of your father the devil, and you love to do the evil things he does. He was a murderer from the beginning. He has always hated the truth, because there is no truth in him. When he lies, it is consistent with his character; for he is a liar and the father of lies.* (John 8:44 NLT).

In three, short sentences, Jesus calls Satan *the devil, an evil doer, murderer, truth hater, liar,* and *the father of lies.* Pretty potent, both in message and choice of audience! And why teach his disciples to pray "lead us not into temptation, but deliver us from the evil one (Matthew 6:13 NIV)," if we don't need to be concerned about this Satan? Why, on the road to the cross would he use up precious breath to pray for them, and us: "My prayer is not that you take them out of the world, but that you protect them from the evil one," (John 17:15 NIV) if it's not important?

Jesus isn't the one confused here, so you can cast this force as bogus to the story of God if you wish – but watch your back. The liar, by nature, lies. He comes disguised to stand out like light or beauty, or meld into the background like a wallflower. Satan's best offensive tactic is hiding in plain sight, disguised as whatever works best to twist God's plans for you. I paid no attention, and it gave Satan the chance he needed, despite my neurotic hypervigilance toward self-protection, to lodge arrows in my heart that I would blame on self, others, or God for four decades.

Back to the opening of Job's drama and the glimpse into the throne room it poses, I wonder if Jesus knew of conversations in the courtroom of God, of requests by Satan to break his own strong heart? If he did, we don't know about it. What we do know is that he, like Job, tested pure at every flaming arrow the enemy shot. Even when understanding, logic, theory, science, and flesh fail, and they will, Jesus, like Job, believed that God was good and could be trusted. And that is a journey we all face as we move closer to the cross and further from all that makes worldly, logical sense.

LOVE WINS
God's certainty about his experiment grew when Jesus completed the human experiment with his love for God intact. He lived a life without missing the mark, made what God said to him more important than his own intelligence, was wary of his capital "E" Enemy, and didn't trust even the cheering crowds around him, "for he knew all people. He did not need any testimony about mankind, for he knew what was in each person. (John 2:24-25 NIV)." *Jesus was not naïve.*

In an ultimate act of trust (and defiance of his Enemy), he was obedient to death, scorning the shame of his execution (Hebrews 12:2), reserved for low-life criminals.

And if we can get past all our modern scorn at things that can't be empirically proven, we'll see Satan's end is pre-planned:

> *Then I heard a loud voice shouting across the heavens, "It has come at last—salvation and power and the Kingdom of our God, and the authority of his Christ. For the accuser of our brothers and sisters has been thrown down to earth—the one who accuses them before our God day and night* (Revelation 12:10 NLT).
> *Then the devil, who had deceived them, was thrown into the fiery lake of burning sulfur, joining the beast and the false prophet. There they will be tormented day and night forever and ever* (Revelation 20:10 NLT).

Someday, Satan will no longer have the access to the throne room – the same access that allowed him to accuse Job, or me, or you. Some of you are skeptical, I get that. But faith is not faith because you see everything. It's faith precisely because you can't see. You have to put down all your arguments and defenses against what Scripture calls, "the knowledge of God (2 Corinthians 10:5)." It's in you, this knowledge. It's in every single beating heart on the planet (Romans 1:20). You just have to cross a line between the physical world and the spiritual. Then your eyes will be open to discern spiritual things. Paul put it like this:

> *But people who aren't spiritual can't receive these truths from God's Spirit. It all sounds foolish to them and they can't understand it, for only those who are spiritual can understand what the Spirit means* (1 Corinthians 2:14 NLT).

It certainly doesn't mean that if you've have crossed that line you suddenly understand everything. I only wish that were so! It simply means that you can accept certain truths by faith, and these truths can begin to guide your life.

One of these guiding truths can be traced back to the beginning of the Big Story of God: We are *imago dei*, made in the image of our Creator. Not so we *become* gods, which might be our inclination, but so we might rule and bring life by imitating our God: his capacity for wholeness and relationship and love; his fire for justice and longing for mercy; a passion that drives us away from loneliness toward relational unity, peace, and love. God breathed his life into us, hoping we would love him for making us so much more than dust. It follows that the Accuser, who pits himself against God, would hate anything that looked, acted, or tasted like God.

Forgetting there is another player committed to defacing the image-bearers of God, even attempting to deface God himself through accusation is a great strategic error in the journey of faith. Let the story of Job, and the arc of the whole story of God convince you that you have indeed been target practice for the Enemy. But take heart, God does not leave us who've crossed the line into faith, even if we're wounded and bleeding.

The eyes of the Lord range throughout the earth to strengthen those whose hearts are fully committed to him.
2 Chron. 16:9 NIV

Chapter 2: Target Practice
QUESTIONS FOR REFLECTION

Question: We typically think of God accusing, especially if we've encountered abuse and come to believe it was our fault. What do you think of the story of Job, particularly the part where God's adversary accuses God of favoritism, claiming that Job only loves God because he is protected?

Question: If God made it all and owns it all and loves it all, does God have just cause to test our hearts to see if we love him back? (Sin against us is *not* a test. Sin against us is harm which God didn't plan but can redeem.)

Question: Could your own story have anything to do with a war between God and his adversary?

Question: Name a scene in your story where Satan may have disguised himself to twist God's plans for you:

Something to ponder: We tend to blame God when bad things happen. Could it affect the way you see your story if you saw your life as a target for Satan, and trusted God to redeem every dark intention that took life from you?

Action: Do your own word study of what Jesus said about the adversary of God. A simple Bible app like biblegateway.com you can look up the same scriptures I did in whatever version you prefer. Write down all the names and purposes that Jesus ascribed to evil. Compare it to your own active beliefs (how you live what you believe) and note the differences.

There's a good God who created good things
and he didn't make us puppets dangling on heaven's string,
and for that there is sometimes hell to pay and
he might not give us answers, but he will give us faith.

And the truth is I don't know the desperate,
lonely places you will need to go
for which there are no answers
but the end to what you know
and a hard fought faith in God
in this world...

April 2017

Chapter 3
Finding *Life* on Planet Earth

*Watch out for people who try to dazzle you with big words
and intellectual double-talk. They want to drag you off into
endless arguments that never amount to anything. They
spread their ideas through the empty traditions of human
beings and the empty superstitions of spirit beings.
But that's not the way of Christ.*
Colossians 2:8 MSG

As a child I learned the story of the emperor who had no
clothes. It's amazing how often that little story floats up for
me today. Looking back, I see how I've resembled the
gullible emperor, blindly trusting whatever the

hoodwinking tailor wanted to tell me, parading around the streets in what turned out to be an embarrassing reveal. More often these days, I see culture in that role, naively proceeding toward greater and greater disaster. Petulantly holding onto the right to do and be and explore whatever whim suits best. Trying on "truth" that changes constantly. The culture preaches, and its preaching is pervasive and constant, like a river seeking to overrun us, a sweeping agenda that isn't even ours, and certainly isn't God's.

In the big picture, being naïve to culture's sermon is simply not wise. Being innocent, or harmless, or virtuous is different. But naiveté is being afraid of the truth or avoiding it because denial suits you better. Throughout the Big Story of God, there has been a clear line between what the culture deems "progress" and what God says about it. The journey toward truth, a.k.a. "spiritual progress," is nothing new, and neither is the journey toward the world's definition of "progress" and "truth." Several thousand years ago, the writer of most of the New Testament and a pastor, Paul, put it like this to his understudy:

> *You should know this, Timothy, that in the last days there will be very difficult times. For people will love only themselves and their money. They will be boastful and proud, scoffing at God, disobedient to their parents, and ungrateful. They will consider nothing sacred. They will be unloving and unforgiving; they will slander others and have no self-control. They will be cruel and hate what is good. They will betray their friends, be reckless, be puffed up with pride, and love pleasure rather than God. They will act religious, but they will reject the power that could make them godly. Stay away from people like that!* (2 Timothy 3:1-5 NLT)

GOSPEL TRUTH

God's agenda for the entire course of history is to help creation flourish. Progress in God's eyes involves not just humans, but the whole earth flourishing. God's long pursuit (described in Chapter 1) is about restoring his original intent in creation:

> *God created human beings; he created them godlike, Reflecting God's nature. He created them male and female. God blessed them: "Prosper! Reproduce! Fill Earth! Take charge! Be responsible for fish in the sea and birds in the air, for every living thing that moves on the face of Earth."*
> Genesis 1:27-28 MSG

He proceeded to make himself knowable in a whole variety of ways: walking and talking with Adam and Eve in the cool of a garden, a perfect creation; then after his hope for them is shattered, delivering and shaping an entire people who will represent him to the rest of the world; then, after his hope for them is shattered, taking on flesh in the person of Jesus to represent himself as clearly as possible to us (Colossians 1:15 and Hebrews 1:3).

Jesus is God's final solution to making himself knowable.

So, you see, God's agenda for you is to really *know* him. Not know all the answers you are seeking to know. Know God. Not know yourself perfectly and completely and build yourself up with education and skills that define who you want to be. Know God. Listen for his Word and purposes in your life. Not use your strength to protect your life and choices and secrets and success and reputation. Know God. "Apprehend" why you've been "apprehended" (Philippians 3:12 KJV) well enough that you see the truth of who He is and who you are. Only then, after the transformational moment when you see who you are before God and fall flat on your face, can you rise again, ready to allow God to define life and where it can be found. Not because you suddenly dishonor your life and strength and skills and passions – but because you finally honor the one who wired you more than yourself. You honor him by *knowing* him.

> *God's Message: "Don't let the wise brag of their wisdom. Don't let heroes brag of their exploits. Don't let the rich brag of their riches. If you brag, brag of this and this only: That you understand and know me. I'm God, and I act in loyal love. I do what's right and set things right and fair, and delight in those who do the same things. These are my trademarks." God's Decree.* (Jeremiah 9:23-24 MSG)

Unfortunately, the Big Story of God does not often unfold with people falling on their faces before him. Over and over in Old Testament narratives, it starts with people raising their fists at him. Then comes the fall, the days of brokenness and distress when clarity comes. To God, we must seem oh-so-predictable:

> *There you will worship man-made gods of wood and stone, which cannot see or hear or eat or smell. But if from there you seek the Lord your God, you will find him if you seek him with all your heart and with all your soul. When you are in distress and all these things have happened to you, then in later days you will return to the Lord your God and obey him.* Deuteronomy 4:28-30 (NIV)

THE GOSPEL ACCORDING TO CULTURE

Before the day of distress, we like to worship wood and stone. Wood in the form of land, resources, edifices erected in our own honor. There are never enough monuments. Stone in the form of solidity and security, thinking we cannot be moved. We don't believe ourselves vulnerable, and spend our days making ourselves even less so.

Western culture preaches that there is no real truth except our own. The 'god within' offers absolute freedom in choices, desires, and paths to whatever utopia I chase. Perhaps science is that path, the "stone" you worship, offering the only answers you can call true. And when scientific evidence changes (as it must due to the nature of scientific discovery) science will again offer a new answer, a new solution you put your faith in.

Perhaps you chase life by becoming "right," ruthlessly intelligent, or by making art and music, running with the popular crowd, looking hot, attaching to a highly significant other, eradicating unpredictability (having control), becoming wealthy, throwing off all convention and starting something new. There are practically as many variations as there are people.

Western culture's dominant message can be summed up in one word: *more*. We buy in to the millions of marketing messages around us: If a little is good, a lot is better. More apps, more advice, more widgets, more types of toothpaste, cereal, packaging, hair color – variety. More products for pampered pets. Bigger, better ATVs, SUVs, RVs, Humvees.

It's as if, in order to validate their existence, companies, institutions and even governments must always produce something new. Something that makes the last thing obsolete. Since I've been either an observer or participant in American business, I've watched workers struggle to make sense of the pace of change. And it's only gotten faster as the information superhighway blows into homes and places of work and worship with alarming speed and our equally alarming accommodation. In my experience, there was rarely time to talk or learn in corporate or non-profit America already 25 years ago. You just tried to keep moving and hoped you were making good decisions – because if you weren't moving fast enough or making good enough decisions, there would be someone close on your heels who would likely be sitting in your chair after you missed a beat.

If you feel that or are living it, you will see the gospel message stands in stark contrast. God has all the time in the world. He doesn't need big, or grandiose or even perfect, because his power starts small and permeates. He creates the world out of nothing, *creatio ex nihilo*, with his word. His economy is generous, yet he doesn't need much to make it so: a grain of salt, a ray of light, a seed that falls into the ground, a baby, a tithe, a talent, a rib, five loaves and two fish that feed 5000, an uneducated fisherman who becomes the leader of the early Christian movement, a teenage boy who kills the giant with a small stone, a teenage girl who says "yes" to God's proposal that she become the mother of the savior of the world.

The Christian Gospel is great news for anyone who feels tired, or small, or broken, or not enough: Little is much in God's hands. We get to rest because we're not pulling the load alone:

> *Then Jesus said, "Come to me, all of you who are weary and carry heavy burdens, and I will give you rest. Take my yoke upon you. Let me teach you, because I am humble and gentle at heart, and you will find rest for your souls. For my yoke is easy to bear, and the burden I give you is light."* (Matthew 11:28-30 NLT)

Culture preaches life is found when we become the master of our own fate and take control of our own destiny. And yet, it's a treacherous game. If we throw out a moral compass based on right and wrong according to God, we fall prey to whomever and whatever makes the best pitch. We follow our bliss until we wake up enslaved to what we thought was freedom. Peter, Jesus' disciple who, after many stumbles became a pastor and leader in the early church, talked about culture's messages and the "false prophets" who spout them like this:

> *They mouth empty, boastful words and, by appealing to the lustful desires of the flesh, they*

> *entice people who are just escaping from those who live in error. They promise them freedom, while they themselves are slaves of depravity—for "people are slaves to whatever has mastered them."*
> 2 Peter 2:18-19 NIV

There are many reasons people buy – and are mastered by – the cultural gospel. It may be all they ever heard or saw in their family of origin. Or, like me, they may have seen faith twisted by sin and concluded that people who follow God are untrustworthy. Maybe God disappointed them, or the church hurt them; perhaps they tried the God-way and it didn't get them where they want to go, or isn't getting them there fast enough. Maybe they simply perceive control and keeping all their options open as perfect ways to be in charge of getting life wherever they can find it, absolving them of responsibility for the methods used to get there.

One side of "absolute freedom" is exercised choosing to become hardened in hopelessness, pushing away longing for anything better, killing desire with despair, addiction, running away, giving up – believing those choices are the only way to cope with life, the only way to survive when culture's gospel, or God, has failed.

And on and on it goes. Finding yet another substitution for the gritty work of needing to trust a God you cannot see and cannot control. A God who has an agenda for your life, who waits patiently for you to finally turn toward him. A God who wants you to flourish with meaning and purpose, to live in the company of people who are safe and trustworthy, to thrive in relationship with Jesus who says, *I am Life* (John 14:6) and *I have come so you can have life, and have it to the full* (Jn 10:10).

One of the primary reasons I worship is because I see God in miraculous terms: so intelligent, so creative, so exceptional, so incredibly amazing that 1) he can take any strategy or work of evil, and bring redemption out of it, and

2) he never gives up. Although he must change his strategy with every new move of Satan and his assistants, he will outwit and outmaneuver the father of lies every time. Only a God like this is able to deliver us from the ways evil has trampled, maimed, defaced, and attempted to devour what belongs to him. I could never do that and I don't believe any human can! But Jesus says there is a particular path for who would step into this life:

> *Enter through the narrow gate. For wide is the gate and broad is the road that leads to destruction, and many enter through it. But small is the gate and narrow the road that leads to life, and only a few find it.* Matthew 7:13-14 NIV

Jesus is talking about a road less traveled versus the broad cultural freeway. He was certainly no stranger to that broad road; around him are the cultural messages of the Jews and the Romans, the latter occupying and ruling the land of his birth. The Jewish spiritual leaders say that following a system of laws and rituals gives life. The Roman and Greek thinkers offer ideas from strict asceticism to total indulgence to find life. To make it all more complicated, the Jewish leaders adopt ideas from the Romans, and vice-versa. Not too different from the church today – a mishmash of strict laws and moral self-determination, of conservative and liberal, of noisy gongs and clanging cymbals. You just find a church that supports whatever you happen to believe and go with it.

Jesus doesn't sit in the lotus position and postulate on the meaning of life. And he doesn't add a bunch of new burdens to people by generating new laws. He looks you in the eye and says, "I am God, wrapped in flesh, and I represent God perfectly." Then, having established his identity (which God backs up, Matthew 3:17 and 17:5, Mark 1:11 and 9:7, and Luke 3:22 and 9:35), he tells story after story explaining God in simple terms: a good shepherd or generous farmer, a landowner, a seed, a treasure, a patient father.

BECOMING OUR OWN MORAL AUTHORITIES

All the way back in the Garden of Eden, choices were offered revolving around fruit from the tree of the knowledge of good and evil (Genesis 2:9). There, culture and gospel, which were once in agreement, fractured as Adam and Eve assumed moral authority rather than trusting it to God. We do the same when we write or rewrite the commandments: Perhaps I should steal if it gets me a better life; perhaps I should lie since the government doesn't deserve this money; perhaps I should steal because I'm smart enough to get away with it. We become elevated in our own thinking and power. Sounds suspiciously like the last verse of Judges, doesn't it? Everyone just does whatever seems right in their own eyes (Judges 21:25).

God becomes nothing more than a cosmic killjoy; we become certain we possess a better plan than his (his would involve us submitting to his ways and requests). The dilemma of the Garden of Eden is the same as ours today: Will I trust what God has said about who I am, about my identity as his son or daughter, about what I should and shouldn't do? Or will I elevate myself above all that and try to "help" God? Or outthink or outwit God? This is a real and present temptation that comes to each of us.

> *Transgression speaks to the wicked deep in his heart; there is no fear of God before his eyes. For he flatters himself in his own eyes that his iniquity cannot be found out and hated.* Psalm 36:1-2, ESV

I became so convinced of my good intentions that I couldn't detect my 'missing of the mark.' But Scripture promises, and I have been the recipient, that when we walk in the light of God, it gives life; and like the sweetest epiphany, walking in light we get even more light as that Psalm promises a few verses later. This is where life is found: *For with you is the fountain of life; in your light do we see light* (Psalm 36: 9 ESV).

People whom God created and loves are still hiding – and from what? From exposure of that light. From loss of control. From the claim of someone larger on their lives. From holding Jesus' eye when he says, *I am God, wrapped in flesh, and have come so you can begin to know God again. You can trust me, and you can follow me to find out where and what life really is.*

COURAGE REQUIRED

It takes courage to lay down all the ways you've tried to find life on your own and begin to look at what God says, but in my recovery from abuse and all the ways it played out into my life and decisions, I became convinced that even in exposure, I could trust God's intentions. Like the prophet Micah said of fumbling, stumbling Israel: The same God who administers correction is the one who is my defense attorney.

> *Though I have fallen, I will rise. Though I sit in darkness, the Lord will be my light. Because I have sinned against him, I will bear the Lord's wrath, until he pleads my case and upholds my cause. He will bring me out into the light; I will see his righteousness.* (Micah 7:8-9 NIV)

The gullible emperor, whom I spoke of at the beginning of this chapter, lacked courage. The courage to have a different opinion than the fast-talking tailor, the courage to call a spade a spade when he looked in the mirror. It actually took a small child to burst the emperor's denial bubble. A child who had no filters when it came to speaking truth. Children are good like that. My little ones helped me see life with clarity many times.

Courage is the bedrock of faith. It takes courage each day to believe in the love of an invisible God. To believe there is a plan for your life and it's good, even when you've encountered bad. To trust what God has said about you and to you. To allow yourself to rely on God's presence when the chips are down and the dark surrounds you.

Our culture tries to define courage as forging ahead, confident in your abilities, but in my mind, true courage is different from believing in my skills, strength, intelligence, or bravery: courage comes from solid faith in God, not self. Within that courage, I believe:

> *I can do all things [which He has called me to do] through Him who strengthens and empowers me [to fulfill His purpose—I am self-sufficient in Christ's sufficiency; I am ready for anything and equal to anything through Him who infuses me with inner strength and confident peace.]* (Philippians 4:13 AMP).

It takes a special kind of courage not to run out and light your own fires when it's dark all around and anxiety is rising. When you don't know God very well and the culture is clamoring, "be more, do more, aim higher – be positive! You can do this!" It's the hardest thing in the world to drop back into the pocket like a good quarterback, waiting for the opening *God* must make for you. You have to trust God sees the entire playing field and knows where you need to move next.

In my anxiety and impatience, I wanted to prove myself to *everyone*, God included. I tried the route of believing in my own wits, power, and strength. Even wanting to impress God, I've tried to be the hero of the story, the savior of others, the redeemer of what went wrong in my own story. Anything but doing the gritty work of vulnerability: trusting God with my reputation and identity, drawing near, putting my life into his hands to use when and where he will.

Now, I've learned to trust God even in the dark, but then, I just wanted to find whatever light I could:

But now, all you who light fires and provide
yourselves with flaming torches, go, walk in the
light of your fires and of the torches you have set
ablaze. This is what you shall receive from my
hand: You will lie down in torment. Isaiah 50:11 NIV

From the time I walked away from God until the day I
returned, broken and humbled, my torment was real,
largely brought on by my own stubborn desire to prove
myself. I no longer blame God because it is not God who
failed. God knows why I walked, and I've experienced not
only his grace and compassion for my abuse, I've also
experienced how his kindness leads to our turn arounds
(Romans 2:4). The moment I turned toward home (the very
definition of repentance), I found God waiting. Like the
father in Jesus' story of the prodigal son (Luke 15:11-32),
he had a robe wrapped around me and a ring on my finger
the moment we met on that broken road. I belonged,
beautifully, mercifully to his family.

Despite the hard things that happened even after my
return, I will never regret leaving culture's sermon behind;
I traded in a pigpen for a palace. I found faith. Freedom.
Worth. Life. I gained a sense of perspective as I began
trusting that what I see is not all there is. And finding life
on earth isn't all there is either. This life I was offered goes
on into an even better forever, something only a Big God
could promise.

So we're not giving up. How could we! Even though on the
outside it often looks like things are falling apart on us, on
the inside, where God is making new life, not a day goes by
without his unfolding grace. These hard times are small
potatoes compared to the coming good times, the lavish
celebration prepared for us. There's far more here than
meets the eye. The things we see now are here today, gone
tomorrow. But the things we can't see now will last forever.
2 Corinthians 4:16-18 MSG

Question: How do being naïve and being harmless or innocent differ in your own mind?

Question: Write your own definition of the world's theory of progress and God's idea of same. Where are they alike and where are they different?

Question: Can you describe a moment in your life when you knew without a shadow of a doubt that God was God and you were not? What was that moment like, and what results flowed out of it?

Question: How are you experiencing the "more and bigger is better" rhythm? By contrast, how does the idea that God "doesn't need big, grandiose or even perfect because his power starts small and permeates" hit you?

Question: If you believed God is really capable of taking anything thrown at him – by evil or by the will of humans – that God has every contingency to bring good out of evil, would it change the way your faith (or your fear) looks?

Action: Have a scavenger hunt. Look for signs of the culture and its message that more and bigger is better (if you have kids, get them to help). How many pictures can you come back with after a couple of hours? Then, set out again looking for signs of God's ideas about how life or progress or truth is defined. Use your pictures to journal about both experiences.

He's standing in a river holdin' on to a pebble,
It's his favorite rock, He never lets it go, and
He's got dreamy eyes as the fireflies
turn into shooting stars
Another day is done; it's time
to make tomorrow's sun

This is our Father, and he is larger,
so much larger than this life
The river flows from beneath His throne, and
The rock He holds we call our home.
Yet He planned our birth and He knows our name
And He says we're worth all the cross became
Oh, He's so much more than maker of heaven and earth –
This is our Father.

August 2006

Chapter 4
Big God

Job answered God: "I'm convinced: You can do anything and everything. Nothing and no one can upset your plans. You asked, 'Who is this muddying the water, ignorantly confusing the issue, second-guessing my purposes?' I admit it. I was the one…I admit I once lived by rumors of you; now I have it all firsthand—from my own eyes and ears! I'm sorry—forgive me. I'll never do that again, I promise!"
Job 42:2-6 MSG

The story Chapter 1 opens with, Job's sorrowful tale of becoming fodder for a disagreement between God and Satan, draws to a close when Job learns more about God firsthand in a strange and breathtaking conversation; God asks the questions and Job is asked to provide answers.

Using this strange method, God never actually answers Job's questions, he just makes it clearer and clearer who he is and of what he is capable. So clearly and passionately does he defend his position as Big God, using five chapters of the narrative to do so, that Job begins to understand more about himself by contrast. Perspective is a funny thing.

Not all of us will get the chance to hear God speak like Job did, but we do each have chances to encounter the bigness of God. Those encounters have the power to change our perspective of God, of ourselves, and of the place of worship in the Big Story.

God's invitation to humans throughout history is to draw near (James 4:8), test him in his generosity (Malachi 3:10), wrestle with him (Job 13:15), trust him to make something good out of the bad things that have happened (Genesis 50:20), rely on him when it's dark and there is absolutely no light (Isaiah 50:10), walk with him (Micah 6:8), and talk with him (Matthew 6:6). It's about God's jealous love, and wanting to be loved and honored in return:

> *You must worship no other gods, for the Lord, whose very name is Jealous, is a God who is jealous about his relationship with you.* (Exodus 34:14 NLT)

HOW DOES GOD *FEEL*?

I think we sometimes put God in a "perfect box" to the point of making him like a robot – no feelings, only rules and code to follow. But that completely removes the jealous lover that I have seen described. Among stories that haunt, there is one in particular that feels like the saddest four verses in the Bible to me. If you can take a moment to look at this story from God's perspective, to put yourself in God's shoes, it will do wonders for your heart of worship.

In this story, it's been 30 days since God parted a sea so the Hebrews could walk across it on dry ground and witness the fate of their pursuers. The waters close in on an entire army. God has heard their cries and provided delivery from slavery with their possessions intact, light in the darkness, protection in the day, food from heaven that falls outside each tent, and capable leadership for this journey. Now, God invites them to come to the bottom of Mount Sinai so he can talk to them:

> *When the people saw the thunder and lightning and heard the trumpet and saw the mountain in smoke, they trembled with fear. They stayed at a distance and said to Moses, "Speak to us yourself and we will listen. But do not have God speak to us or we will die." Moses said to the people, "Do not be afraid. God has come to test you, so that the fear of God will be with you to keep you from sinning." The people remained at a distance, while Moses approached the thick darkness where God was.*
> Exodus 20:18-21

Wait a minute! Where is their love? Appreciation? Devotion? At the very least, when God asks you to come near wouldn't you do it because you're scared *not* to? Apparently not the people God himself has named "wrestles with God!" Although he has invited them, they don't even want to hear the sound of his voice. I can feel the pain of betrayal in that verse. And, although God knows this conversation is important to their *perspective* (who he is and who they are). Drawing near will inoculate them against missing the mark. But they retreat rather than risk. They remain at a distance, afraid for their lives before the one who has rescued them, and the Big Story of God suffers another chapter of rejection. It makes me want to cry and rail over the injustice of only Moses getting the relationship with God we were each meant to have.

Do you dare to draw near to a God who might frighten you with his immensity or intensity, one who invites you near enough so you have proper perspective on your sin and his holiness, one who might shape and change your cherished habits and desires, and shake you out of your lesser stories into his bigger one? One who could transform you from pleading *not* to hear his voice for fear you will die, to one who longs for *even one word* from his storehouse of wisdom, kindness, compassion, righteousness, justice? If you understood that a full conversation with God could inoculate you against the temptations that assail your heart and mind each day, would you draw near, scorning the thunder and lightning and smoke?

I had been in church all of my life until I walked away at age 30, unwilling to hear his voice – to draw near to the fire and thunder. But encountering God's amazing rescue at age 43 toppled the throne I had given to idols. I began to see the immense and holy Big God pursuing broken me with an offer of friendship. It caused a *worship response*. I couldn't help myself.

What difference would it make to you if you actually believed, in practice, that God is the pursuer of friendship with you; that Jesus isn't just spouting trite phrases when he says, "Come to me, all of you who are weary and carry heavy burdens, and I will give you rest (Matthew 11:28 NLT)." And what if the Holy Spirit gives not only breath, but the very essence of life? If you knew that you could find what your soul is most thirsty for in worship, would you come in the same way you do now? Would you begin to seek worship, communication with the true and living God, rather than entertainment, comfort, pleasure, escape?

THE DISCONNECT

All I'm saying here is I often see a disconnect between The Big Story of God and the lesser stories of how we seek God in our own lives. If your God is small, your worship will also be. If your God is The God of the Big Story, your worship will follow. So, what kind of God do you believe in? Small and ineffectual? Capricious? Selfish? One in need of worship to bolster his self-esteem? And where do you truly find life (and I don't just mean breath here)? What do you reach for when you're tired, out-of-sorts, and empty — a caffeinated soft drink? *Really?*

There is irony in a culture that implies we can find refreshment, relaxation, and renewal by reaching for a 'moment.' Even in worship, the 'moment' can become a search for some*thing* to provide momentary relief: the right instrument, the right groove, the right personality in the pulpit, the right-looking family, and dear God, please don't let that weirdo talk to me. I'm convinced we don't need to live for *the moment*. We need to reach for the promises.

Maybe it's time to look again at the God we believe in and what he's saying. Maybe it's time to hear again that in worship, we are actually responding to an invitation rather than fulfilling an obligation or tradition. That distant song we are drawn toward is his song. The ancient, passionate, never-ending heartbeat of a God who has longings too. Longings for real, authentic relationship with us:

> *The Lord your God is in the midst of you, a Mighty One, a Savior [Who saves]! He will rejoice over you with joy; He will rest [in silent satisfaction] and in His love He will be silent and make no mention [of past sins, or even recall them]; He will exult over you with singing.* Zephaniah 3:17 AMP

GOD'S RESPONSE TO THE TRUTH ABOUT HUMANS

This God we worship is the same God who saw the people he loved just couldn't be faithful to their promises. But instead of wiping them out, he cut a new covenant *with himself* to love no matter how we responded (Genesis 9:8-11; Genesis 15:18; Exodus 34:10; Jeremiah 31:31-34; Luke 22:19-20). In ancient times, the strength in a covenant lay in the fact that both parties were willing to die to keep it. In Jesus, the Triune God fulfilled every covenant he made.

This is a big God, capable of creating worlds with just words. A God with enough heart to love what he created, and enough strength to go after what he lost in the fall. A God passionate enough about keeping promises that he is willing to go to war, even die, to keep them.

We are his pearl of great price. Grabbing hold of that truth alone can change our worship. Be willing to enlarge your view of God, and your worship will follow.

Whenever I serve as a worship leader, I am challenged by the reality that there is a worship service already in progress when we begin (Revelation 4). Rather than creating 'worship' with *our* efforts, we are invited to co-create with a Triune God in a cathedral without ceilings, to join in songs that have been sung since the morning stars sang together at the dawn of creation (Job 38:4-7). Invited not just to hear the word of God from scripture, but to be aware that *the Word of God is with us* (John 1:1-6), reminding us again that no one knows the Father like he does. He's willing on the one hand, to keep explaining the Father's heart to us, and on the other, to keep explaining our hearts to the Father. This is his role as the perfect priest, prayer warrior and advocate (Luke 22:31-32, Romans 8:26-28 and 8:34, 1 Timothy 2:5, 1 John 2:1, Hebrews 7:25 and 9:24, Job 16:19, and Isaiah 53:12) – and while we may hear the echo of this melody in our centers of worship today, I wonder if we might move a little closer to the source?

Jesus is very much alive, fighting for us, inviting us to a relationship with the Father; showing us the way through the torn curtain as the better worship leader of the church (Hebrews 2:12). Sharing himself, the Word of God, through the breaking of bread and drinking of cup. Reminding us forgiveness and grace and understanding are ours, bought and paid for by him.

I don't believe we can come to worship looking for a 'moment,' and experience all that God has for us. That would be like accepting a bag of Pop Rocks in lieu of a trip to the Grand Canyon. Sure, Pop Rocks surprise and entertain your mouth, but the Grand Canyon gulfs and dwarfs and brings sudden awe. Perspective.

Similarly, we come to marriage looking for a relationship, not a 'moment;' companionship in both the ups and downs of life, good and bad, sickness and health. What kind of marriage just exists when times are perfect? Christ loved the church enough to die *before there even was* a church, and he has continuously offered relationship to each member of his body, the Body of Christ, since then – through the comfort and counsel of the Holy Spirit, and through his ongoing role as high priest and mediator:

> *Therefore He is able also to save to the uttermost (completely, perfectly, finally, and for all time and eternity) those who come to God through Him, since He is always living to make petition to God and intercede with Him and intervene for them.*
> Hebrews 7:25 AMP

Imagine, wives, the joy of a husband who lived to run interference for you whenever you needed it, prayed for you non-stop, listened to your groans too deep for words and translated them into language you both can understand! Imagine husbands, the joy of a wife who trusted you completely and always came to you with questions, doubts, concerns and praise in a posture of absolute confidence that you had the perfect word for her! This is the relationship Jesus offers us not only personally, but through the Body of Christ. There we have companionship in the ups and downs of life. And through his Spirit, we have a seal of promise that *we are never* and *will never be* left alone (John 14:16).

STOP PRETENDING

But something is required, and it's something we have a hard time being in worship. It's called being real. Yes, we are moving toward holiness, but that is not a call to pretend we are holy. Even Paul, writer of well over half of the New

Testament, missionary-extraordinaire, Jesus-transformed, and sainted-after-death, says:

> *I don't mean to say that I have already achieved these things or that I have already reached perfection. But I press on to possess that perfection for which Christ Jesus first possessed me.* Phil 3:12 NLT

Jesus only really teaches about worship once in his ministry, at least according to our scriptures. Yes, he quotes the Old Testament about worshipping God alone to the religious folks and the devil, but he *teaches* on worship *only once*. In passing, he says that you can't worship both God and money. And in passing he says that God hears the prayers of those who truly worship him and do his will. But he reserves his "worship sermon" for a woman married and divorced five times, shacking up with a sixth man, and embarrassingly alone at a well in the middle of the day (John 4).

What do we learn from this unlikely conversation with a woman most people want to pretend away – especially in the church?

We learn that God is seeking. God is seeking real people with real lives who will stop arguing about who he is and worship in spirit and in truth. Men and women who will let the masks fall and allow God's light into the dark chambers of their stories. If we only heard an echo of that haunting melody, our worship would change. God seeks. God invites us to his table. We are wanted, desired, and exulted over with singing, regardless of our past or present circumstances. Whether we carry the scars of shame or the disdainful pride of perfectionism, worshipping in truth is powerful: the truth of who God is, and the truth about us, naked and unadorned before our Maker. Grand Canyon perspective. We aren't sought because of what we can do for God's reputation. And we aren't saved by grace so we can subject ourselves to ruthless perfectionism:

Let me put this question to you: How did your new life begin? Was it by working your heads off to please God? Or was it by responding to God's Message to you? Are you going to continue this craziness? For only crazy people would think they could complete by their own efforts what was begun by God. If you weren't smart enough or strong enough to begin it, how do you suppose you could perfect it? Did you go through this whole painful learning process for nothing? It is not yet a total loss, but it certainly will be if you keep this up!
Galatians 3:3-4 MSG

We are sought, not for our treasure but because we are treasured. That is a place of respect, dignity, good and meaningful purpose and work, and the enjoyment of resting in our position rather than striving to get to the next level as if we were trapped in a video game. This is more than a 'moment;' it's a marriage. An invitation to freedom, peace and joy that awakens our souls and spirits to the Big Story of a Big God.

We can't help but worship in spirit when we catch the truth. And it shows up in all of life…and all of life becomes worship.

I'm the only God there is— The only God who does things right and knows how to help.
So turn to me and be helped—saved!— everyone, whoever and wherever you are. I am God, the only God there is, the one and only. I promise in my own name: Every word out of my mouth does what it says. I never take back what I say.
Everyone is going to end up kneeling before me.
Everyone is going to end up saying of me,
'Yes! Salvation and strength are in God!'"
Isaiah 45:21-23 MSG

Chapter 4: Big God
QUESTIONS FOR REFLECTION

Question: Write about an opportunity you've had to encounter the bigness of God – how did it change your perspective of God, yourself, or worship?

Question: Respond to the thought that God could feel betrayal in the same way you might feel betrayal when someone you love spurns you: Has God ever felt betrayed by you? Have you ever felt betrayed by God?

Question: If you knew that you could find what your soul is most thirsty for in worship, would you come in the same way you do now? How would that knowledge affect how you spend your time?

Something to ponder: What if holiness is more wrapped up with how big God is rather than how perfect we can be? What if gaining a bigger perspective of Big God helps rid us of the sins that constantly dog us? Would it be worth drawing nearer?

Action: If you are able, try a hospitality experiment. Invite a few people to dinner. Notice the way you feel when the invitation is accepted. Notice the way you feel if someone says "no," or doesn't respond to your invitation. Afterward, journal about it and try to put yourself in God's shoes as he invites you to his table. Can you accept with joy? Can you rest in being treasured? Would you rather decline, or ignore his invitation? Why or why not?

SECTION 2: BIG QUESTIONS
(At Least as Old as Job)

Inside this secret closet in my heart
Lie all these thoughts best hidden in the dark
Inside a room too lonely for a spark to light a flame
Here I bring failure, longing close behind
Here I bring questions raw and unrefined
Here I hide all you wouldn't want to see
that's part of me

Who would ever come and invite me not to run?
Who would hold my hand and not let go? and
Is there anyone to whom I'd give a key?
And is there any room except for me?

Thru tired walls so filled with cracks and holes
A light has dared to break into my soul
From One whose eyes won't turn away I know,
though others do
He says this closet deep inside of me
Is not as hidden as I'd like it to be
He's always been there waiting tenderly
To unlock this prison door and set me free

He will always come and invites us not to run
He will hold our hands and not let go, and
If there's anyone to whom I'd give a key
It's Him because He's promised to redeem
This secret closet waiting for the light
His flame of truth to enter what I hide
Bring beauty out of ashes from that fire
To offer hope to others such as I

April 2005

60

Chapter 5
What's Wrong with Me? Why Can't I Fly?

You've probably seen those bumper stickers, "I'd rather be flying!" right?

Raised by parents who were both private pilots, I can honestly say if a small plane is the ticket, I'd rather stay home. I loved the thrill of flying, but after the scares, near misses, and arguments about money it caused, I lost enthusiasm.

In my late 20s, I was introduced to hot air ballooning, and it re-captured for me the essence of my childhood dreams of flying like a bird. The breeze against my skin, the incredible views of New England in fall slipping below the gentle basket, sailing close enough to a tree to touch its leaves, and once even dipping my feet into a little country lake. Heavenly. Reminders of all the flying dreams I had as a child – just me with arms outstretched, floating along wherever the wind took me.

Why was the ballooning experience so dear to me? This taste of flying was the closest thing I ever experienced to freedom in real life. Up there, I felt weightless. I knew and trusted the pilot and left behind the worries and tethers that characterized my life on the ground. A confirmed people pleaser by my 30s, I was trying to climb some sort of ladder in my professional life, working 60 or 70 hours a week; caught between a troubled marriage and separation, and a troubling affair that began during my separation.

Now I can see more clearly what I couldn't see then. My drive to please, impress, stand out, push harder and farther and higher was rooted in shame. My penchant to run from conflict and sabotage good was rooted in fear and lies. My desire for freedom was rooted in pain.

All I knew then was I was suffocating. I wanted to live, not die. And so, I ran. I ran as far away from God and church and being a "good girl" as I could. I said these very words: I'm going to take a sabbatical from God; I just don't understand him."

THE SECRET CLOSET

Although I was born into a Christian family, there were many ways, nonetheless, in which my family system was dysfunctional; probably like most homes, Christian or not. But you would hope that in the frequent study of Scripture, the ongoing emphasis of prayer and its importance, and the teaching of morals and ethics so implicit in God's original 10 laws, a family would find healing and wholeness simple.

Yet wholeness seemed to evade our family, despite college-educated parents, faith, and enough money from my Dad's medical practice in dusty West Texas for a plane and some travel. My parents had wounds from their childhood they had never unpacked. They had wounds in their marriage that festered into open conflict, lack of respect toward each other, and passive-aggressive behaviors that slowly wore away at the fabric of relationship. Although they stayed together more than 60 years, I don't think love characterized their marriage. Maybe duty, maybe shame, maybe fear, maybe just a sense that there were no other options. But not true love.

Dr. Dan Allender, one of my favorite authors, would say that abuse is most often found in homes where emptiness characterizes the atmosphere, and that a lack of love (and all the things stable, consistent love nurtures like security, confidence, and personal growth) provides a set up where abuse flows in to fill the vacuum (*The Wounded Heart,* page 93).

My home felt like that. I experienced a level of perfectionism from my mother that always left me feeling insecure, not right, not enough. My father sent me an opposite message: that I was somehow "special," or "unique," a star waiting to be born. Yet he did nothing to draw out or nurture whatever skills, gifts, or talents he might have seen. I felt like a trophy, like a feather in his cap. A child whose job it was to make him look good, but alone in the process of becoming as great as he imagined me to be. He chided me often that I could be Miss America if I applied myself but did nothing to prevent the abuse that undermined the beauty of soul and body.

I gravitated toward my father as a confirmed daddy's girl. His messages of me being special drew me, yet much later realized that our relationship was stamped with a pattern I carried into adulthood – chasing men who were emotionally unavailable. I got his attention as a child and teen, but as an adult, understood that I had done all the work of relationship. He didn't pursue me, I pursued him. I felt empty and alone, even in a big family.

It was polarizing, being caught between believing I was never enough, yet feeling I was supposed to shine and make the family proud. I was the middle child of five, and as pecking orders go, each child feels compelled to carve out a unique space that belongs to them, and the middle children are often afraid of being forgotten. I think I determined that, not only would I not be forgotten, I would stand out in a crowd. Even my name felt like something I needed to live into. My mother was the one who had chosen it and I loved the reasons: Amy was for that bright character from *Little Women*, a beautiful go-getter determined to not be left behind. Louise was for the books' author Louisa May Alcott. I felt destined to be a writer, and started early, writing poems and songs even in elementary school.

I remember the day, as a 6th grader, I made *the sacred vow*. Now, childhood vows are really important, and strangely powerful. If you've ever made any that you're conscious of, you may want to go back and look at how they've steered your life. Mine was to always smile, no matter what was happening around me, and that conviction pretty much drove my life until I fell apart at age 42.

I had three siblings ahead of me, and none of them seemed to have much interest in the idea of being popular. I wanted popularity, to stand out and be "special." I hated it with a passion when a teacher (or some other adult) said things like, "oh here comes another of *those* kids." My oldest brother was mechanical, and a private pilot before he graduated high school. My older sister was brainy, reading by age four, and winning spelling bees. Her nose was always in a book it seemed. My brother ahead of me by three years had a hard time with everything. He was dyslexic, not well-liked, and turned into a super-spiritual Holy Joe by the time he was in junior high. Pity my younger brother, who had to follow all that, plus try to understand the crazy sister determined to be popular!

My vow was about how to appear in school in order to become well-liked; I don't think it necessarily showed up at home. There, I took on the role of peacemaker, particularly between my parents. My mother would tell me at age 85, fighting Alzheimer's and isolated in a nursing home, "Oh, Amy, I love it when you're here, you have a way of smoothing things over between your Dad and me."

I don't say that because I'm proud of it, I say it because she was responding to my 50-year habit of diffusing arguments or tension between them. Think of the effort it takes a child to 1) constantly scan the atmosphere for signs of stress, and 2) make him/herself responsible for peace between adults. But I cut my teeth on those behaviors, sometimes using humor, sometimes sweetness, sometimes distraction to try to make my world feel less chaotic. I could never stand conflict – it threatened to undo me. And so, swallowing what I felt and acting to control what others thought of me became my *modus operandi*.

The textbooks might call it "external locus of control," but I came to think of it as "spinning." The harder I spun, the less the world could see the truth in favor of just a blur; a high-energy girl / woman on a mission. I enjoyed a bit of popularity, mainly resulting in getting elected to positions I had no idea how to fulfill, like vice-president of our student council my senior year. At least as "most humorous" the same year, I didn't really have to know anything to succeed. I was empty, scared, full of ambivalence. Yet the energy to shine and to obscure the truth was plentiful. Ah, the vitality of youth. To push and push and push toward a goal that isn't even good for you!

Somewhere along the way, I lost touch with the truth about me. My early love of people became skepticism; my love of all things creative got shot down. Dancing was not allowed, so ballet (the only legitimate way for a girl to spin!), was out of the question. Art lessons were too expensive or not to be found in my little town. Music was allowed, but anything outside of band, choir, sacred, or classical frowned upon. The real me was drawn to poetry and lyrics and contemporary music. I wrote poetry from age 9 or so and began writing songs with my guitar in high school. Oh, how I dreamed of moving to Nashville and writing songs.

But that was the *inside* me, the girl I hid, whose dreams I nurtured but rarely let anyone else see. Those were tucked away so deeply my own little secret closet that they just about disappeared. Deep inside, I became untrusting of others, including my parents and God, unsure of how and why to trust someone so big who seemed to see me unworthy of protecting. I slipped into a persona, the projection of a happy-go-lucky kid, ready to set the world on fire. I would never show weakness and I would never cry.

These days, the internet has made it so much easier to project whatever image you want others to see, but even in the 60s and 70s, spinning the truth was my coping mechanism. Although I wanted to write songs, I pursued journalism in college, unwilling to risk the real me in order to protect the vulnerable girl inside. Dreams were scary, and dreams that involved words deeply felt on paper, offered to others for critique even scarier! I gravitated toward telling someone else's story. I stayed on the right side of the question-asking, the side where even 'truth' could be worked and reworked; edited and finessed. I stayed on the side of Miss Congeniality, a title I won in two county pageants in high school because I did a good job of being likable.

As nearly as I can recall, the abuse started at about age five, and the final episode occurred about age 16. The secret closet was the place I stored it all. I was 43 before I even called it abuse, so convinced was I that it was my fault somehow. That I was wretched in my sin, or shameful in my beauty.

I think the details of the abuse not as important as the fire it started in my soul. You see, we have a penchant for comparing our own stories of pain and loss to another's.

Sometimes it gives us the right to feel better because someone else had it so much worse; sometimes, it shames us again because our story makes us feel so different and twisted. I know this because I've heard hundreds of stories of survivors of all kinds of abuse.

So, rather than details, I offer the simple truth in a big picture. My abuse was sexual in nature, perpetrated by a close family member over a decade of my young life. There may have been only as many occasions of abuse as number of years it went on, but again, I have come to see that frequency, or even severity, is only one part of the story. The legacy of any abuse, sexual abuse included, is that the victim feels somehow responsible, damaged, shameful, and full of self-doubt. How we handle those feelings, first as children, later as adults, shapes our future.

Yes, the details matter, especially to the soul harmed, but, for others, obsession about details can become just one more way of distancing themselves from the real story. A way to scandalize and provoke fascination but take us away from the heart of the one wounded, or our own heart for that matter. This is why asking a victim about the details of his/her abuse can be experienced as re-traumatizing. "What happened in your heart," is far different than, "what happened next?" The latter becomes about you and your desire to know, not about the person whose boundaries have been violated. A tip if you want to hear stories of abuse: Don't ask for details of the story, ask for a map of the heart behind the story.

I believe, as I look around culture today, that many type-A, driven behaviors on one end of the spectrum, and the twin cultures of depression and self-medication that plague our nation on the other, could have their roots in stories similar to my own. After all, the statistics for sexual abuse during the decade that I unpacked my own suggested that about 28 percent of women and about 8 percent of men in the United States experienced sexual abuse before they were 18, and that's just the ones who reported. It is thought that 62 percent of those abused don't tell, sometimes ever. (The Magnitude of the Problem, 2020, http://www.d2l.org/wp-content/uploads/2017/01/Statistics_1_Magnitude.pdf)

It's easy to conclude, given those numbers that, for people in my generation, between age 50 and 80 let's say, abuse has affected family, gender identification, dating, marriage, parenting, and the journey of faith for millions.

I can't tell their stories; I can only tell mine. I can only tell you that in my emptiness as a child, I used to long for someone to guide me, someone to see my potential and take me under their wing. My father never said anything about the abuse to me, even though he knew at one point; my mother knew and made me feel responsible. I rejected them as people trusted to advise or mentor and moved deeper into the loneliness of the secret closet. Who could I ever let in? I trusted no one, yet in a strange irony I consistently put others in charge of telling me who I was.

I had a longing for peace. I literally wished for world peace every time I blew out birthday candles or threw a penny in a fountain. Not love, or fame, or riches. Peace! I also wanted wisdom, and clearly remember asking God for wisdom like Solomon had – and faithfulness, which in the end, Solomon seemed to lack. Even as a child I was drawn to the wisdom literature of the Bible. If you can imagine a young girl reading the books of Job and Ecclesiastes, that was me.

Job's unfair suffering spoke to me, but like Job, I knew nothing of the deceiver, and how that evil force can work to crush hope. I saw that God allowed Job's suffering for some reason, and it sure didn't make me trust God more. Ecclesiastes, and all of Solomon's observations about the meaning and futility of life seemed more authentic to me than all the surety of Jesus or Paul. My abuser was always spouting off about how he loved Jesus, and my Mom casting out demons and anointing people with oil.

Skepticism toward people who seem sure of themselves is practically woven into my DNA.

At age 59, my perspective on suffering is much more theological than the ponderings of a little girl. But it is that girl that I must go back for; her fear, her vulnerability, her ways of running and spinning. It is her story that I must own, as well as the whole truth about God, in order to find the *shalom* – which literally means not only peace, but also harmony, wholeness, completeness, prosperity, welfare and tranquility. What God intended for each of his children.

My 59-year-old head can get in the way of remembering what it was like to feel dread in the night, or panic when my parents left me alone with my abuser. To feel ugly hatred for him, and myself, when I had to touch his underclothes to hang them out to dry on our clothesline. To feel such intolerable anxiety that I would hit my stomach long into the night, trying to beat out the child that might be living there.

It was probably the second episode of the decade-long saga that found me running to my mother, crying. I told her how my abuser, three years older, had laid on top of me, fully clothed, then told me that's how girls get pregnant. Maybe you could defend him with terms like "childhood exploration," at that point, but I was truly scared out of my mind. Now, I find it inexcusable that my mother didn't try to calm my fears with the truth or even run to reproach my abuser. Then, I just took what she offered, even though it tasted like poison. She led me through a prayer for forgiveness, quietly tying a burden of guilt and shame to my back that I carried for almost four decades. A prayer, forced from my lips, set the trajectory of my belief that I was to blame for what had happened. God might not really know everything, or might be angry and judgmental and intolerant and capricious despite the truth. Maybe I *was* pregnant, and maybe I deserved whatever was coming my way. Mom never tried to clear up the misconception, even though I was only maybe seven years old.

I choked out that 'forgive me,' but my heart recoiled in anguish. Enter ambivalence; enter the war inside where God was the winner, and there was only one, small loser. Me. He was God, but I wasn't sure I liked him, and I was pretty sure he didn't like me.

I don't know if it was months or years that I beat my stomach, but the day it started, the day of *the prayer*, I split in two. There was me, and there was my persona – and the two might live in the same body, but they hardly ever spoke, one pretending to ignore the other. And I can tell you this: I never told my mother again about anything bad that happened to me. An effective wall came down between us that persisted until I was in my 30s, many heartaches later. And I *never* cried.

Looking back, I think it served my mother well to have me believe that I might be pregnant. In her way of thinking, if I was scared of boys, or of sexuality, she could be less concerned about me getting in trouble. Trust me, my mother was not a monster, and part of my story is the healing that took place between us over the decades. But, oh, the cost of her lack of truth and compassion in those early years. The abuse continued, unmolested, so to speak.

I bought the lie that it was my responsibility to not let my femininity be seen or admired. Beauty was dangerous, and my need to be loved and admired became my biggest flaw, the vulnerability that caught me over and over again. It's easy to see how becoming Miss America would have presented problems!

As the years clicked on, I came to hate my neediness, to value control without honesty, to bear pain without letting anyone see. I bought my mother's lies that it was somehow *my* job to protect myself and that men were incapable of containing their lust. Thus, when I failed to protect myself, which I inevitably did, there was no one to blame but me. I believed I was more powerful than I really was, the responsible one who failed. You see, the perpetrator of my abuse didn't need to make me believe it was my fault, my mother did it for him, and then I did it to myself.

My father's silence in the abuse was, in the end, just as damaging as my mother's words. Dad, the hero of my early world, could encourage me to become Miss America, a beautiful face and figure to be adored by the masses. But he didn't have the guts to wade into conflict to rescue or protect the core of who I was. *Silence is violence*, I learned as I faced the damage years later. The lessons I learned from his lack of voice affected my sense of self-value and killed my chances to learn lessons about boundaries and respect between men and women. And his seven words to my abuser (words I never knew about for four decades, and then not from him) were shaming. "Keep your p**** in your own pants," was all he said.

At age 14 or so, I put down a boundary, standing up to my abuser as he tried another tactic to get his way. "No! You can't treat me like this!" I said. He left me alone…for a time.

I formed a passionate attachment to a guy I had met the summer before my freshman year in high school. Perfectly physically unavailable, he lived in British Columbia. We met during a summer missions' outreach that started with training in Florida. After training, I went to Brazil, he to the American West. We got to know each other over the following year through a wonderful letter-writing campaign, sharing secrets, music loves, and verse we had written. In letters, with long distances between us, he was a soulmate, but when I went to visit him in Canada my junior year of high school, the physical presence of relationship rapidly consumed the friendship we had built. After I came home, lengthy collect phone calls into the wee hours ensued. I couldn't pay for them. My parents were angry at me – the peacemaker! I was angry at him, and at myself for falling into needing and being needed. The relationship that had started out wonderful and exciting became suffocating. His need to be convinced of my love, and both our insecurities rose up to kill the spark between us. It ended badly, but my foray into relationships with men, who were in one way or another unavailable, had only begun.

Time passed. I felt powerful and successful in my ability to keep myself safe from my abuser. The clock ticked on, and he left town for college. I relaxed further, feeling the abuse was behind me. But his steps returned one last time and the final episode of abuse was by far the most traumatic. The all-powerful me failed at *my* responsibility to protect myself. How could I *not be to blame* for the horrible person I became, after standing up for myself? He found me alone, offered me a backrub, and before it was over, my maturing body experienced pleasure. Abuse mixed with pleasure was like a bomb going off in my soul.

This blackness, this splintering of self, this failure to protect, this neediness that defiles! *What is wrong with me? I am wrong. I am bad. This is all my fault* came the deafening accusations.

I was almost 50 years old before I could bear to even think of that story, let alone speak of it or process it. As a teen, I didn't understand that God had wired my body to respond. There was nothing wrong with me, there was something wrong with my abuser. In my way of thinking then, however, I was wrong and bad and it was unforgiveable. My abuser never bothered me again in my flesh, but my mind, soul, and spirit were caught in a crucible where pain and pleasure, power and powerlessness, loathing and love, betrayal and trust swirled, almost faster than I could spin.

Still, the *MO* was firmly in place – march on, don't show how you feel – spin, spin, spin for others. Tell their stories, make them feel heard and cared for. Smile when your heart is breaking. Above all, don't let anyone see the ugly truth. Disappear further wounded girl who was, deeper into the secret closet; shine brighter, girl who is leaving you behind.

This, for me, was the threshold from which I entered adulthood. I gathered my dreams of freedom around me and took off with a broken wing and a very nice spin, hoping that, maybe, no one would notice.

Question: Are you aware of any vows you made as a child? Name the ways those have shaped your life. Is it time to leave any of them behind? To revoke the power they have over your adult life?

Question: What was your role in your family of origin, and what was your *modus operandi* to keep yourself "safe" and get to young adulthood?

Question: Did you have any dreams or ways you were wired as a child that you need to remember and re-explore? Did you throw away anything good just to survive?

Question: Think back about what it was like to be a child – do you recognize any experiences or feelings that were at war inside you? Name your ambivalence:

Question: What did you lose because the abuse or trauma that happened to you wasn't handled well? If you could have a do-over, what would change about how it was handled?

Action: Pick just one wound from your childhood that was significant and write a letter to the person who wounded you – not a letter to mail, a letter just for your own sake. Don't overwhelm yourself by trying to tackle everything at once, just one wound, one person. What would you like to say to them if they could say nothing back to defend themselves or shame you? It's important to tell them what their actions did to your heart, not just your body or mind. Heart issues are where behaviors flow from, it's how we get shaped, and where we shut down.

Careful with my nouns, careful with my verbs
Careful with my manners, measured all my words
Weeded out opinions before they got their start
Yeah, I was really careful if you don't count my heart.

I covered it so perfectly that no one stopped to stare
At all the pretty Band-aids I stuck under there
They made a careful picture in which I played my part
Yeah, I was so successful if you don't count my heart

Oh I gave it to thieves who took it for a jewel
To lovers who wanted to play me for a fool, and
I trusted it to idols until they bled me dry
'Cause I didn't know my heart held the source of life

So how do I watch over this river I can't see
That flows with his life in and out of me
Oh it's clear this is a treasure he's given me to guard
But I have been so reckless in matters of my heart

Oh I gave it to thieves who took it for a jewel
To lovers who wanted to play me for a fool, and
I trusted it to idols until they bled me dry
'Cause I didn't know my heart held the source of life

September 2007

Chapter 6
Why Did I Get Hurt? Is This My Fault?

Dang, I loved my freshman year at college!

What's not to love about glorious freedom? My abuser far away at another university. I got a fresh view with no bad memories attached, a way out from under the frustration and resentment that fueled my relationship with my mother during my teen years and the repressive control that ruled all of a childhood where Dad never really used his voice, and Mom was fearful and overprotective.

As a family, we went to church, and that was about the extent of what was allowed. Every few weeks, Mom drove 80 miles to the nearest large city, Lubbock, to shop, get us piano lessons, and just see something different. My parents also had their flying, and I sometimes went for a ride. But for me, life felt small. I was never allowed to go to or have a slumber party, for example, and even spending the night with a friend was a rarity. By the time my peers were having other kinds of parties, I wasn't in the circle to be invited. I avoided a lot of temptation by not being at those parties, but I was definitely social, eager to have friends and be included, and I didn't really have examples in my home of how to develop and nurture good relationships.

My parents had lived in Lubbock from just before my birth until I was four, and Mom really liked to go back there. As a mother of five, maybe there was something to be said for strapping a number of us into the car and spending a day driving, shopping, visiting, and dining out? Anyway, I liked those outings too. I liked the city, and the sense that something bigger and more beautiful was happening in the world than my dusty, little hometown let on to. Oh, and there was also the bakery my mom favored too and its world-class coffee rolls that always found their way into our shopping cart.

When it came time for college, I rethought a decision to attend the college where my parents met; a faith-based, conservative college where I had been admitted to the nursing program. A musical group had invited me to tour with them for the following year and I wanted to stay close to home to raise funds for that experience. In August, I applied to Texas Tech University in Lubbock, where I was pretty sure I would be a shoo-in, and it didn't take but a minute to fall in love with freedom.

My freshman year was one for the books. I danced, drank, flirted, and still managed to do well in my studies. I made good friends and developed as many social acquaintances as I could handle. The vitality of youth (and the 18-year-old drinking age in Texas) allowed me to easily stay up until 2 am, then get up the next morning for a gym class at 7 a.m. I went to church a few Sunday mornings across the street from campus, but it was really just another social gig; maybe a chance to meet some guys.

Even though it was sort of hedonistic, that year became the benchmark for freedom in my mind. As I grappled with the concept of freedom in Christ over the years, that taste of freedom was the fulcrum of my wrestling. Doing what I wanted stood in such stark contrast to always doing what someone else wanted. I felt so alive, so full of fun and joy, and theorized that I never really hurt anyone, expect maybe my parents who were pretty upset when I told them I was drinking and dancing. I'll never forget my dad's reaction to that revelation. He seemed betrayed. It was probably the biggest reaction I ever saw from him that wasn't anger. For the first time, he told me my grandfather had been an alcoholic, and that as a teen, he had gotten out of the car one day, refusing to ride with his father again.

My parents were teetotalers, and I finally began to see them as people beyond their legalistic faith. They had stories of their own and hopes for us kids that had more to do with us avoiding pain than proving our obedience. That truth became key for me in my relationship with God. But, unfortunately, I had to experience a lot of pain before obedience looked remotely attractive.

The year away from college with the touring group was, for me, exhausting. Over the four decades since, I've tried to understand why it hit me that way, when others have such fond memories of our travels together. They still want to get together and party, I just want to stay at home and ponder why I feel so different.

I struggled with depression, far from home and the college experience that had brought such joy. It was a thrill to sing daily in schools, prisons, hospitals, nursing homes, group homes and other places people need hope and cheer– but I felt their challenges deeply, as if they were my own. From this point on in life, I noticed that I couldn't seem to separate myself from others' pain. I felt everything, too much, and my characteristically smiley-girl persona seemed to withdraw. Almost every night the band geared up and the crowds gathered in auditoriums, opera houses, and stadiums. But we sang of the hope of humanism, the power of people to overcome, thrive, and impact the world with optimism. Ah, the dream and illusion of progress. That it's all getting better, and we're the ones doing it. I just never felt that dream, and it depressed and drained me to keep selling it.

Perhaps I was caught between the splintered parts of myself: the introspective muse and the extroverted caretaker, the abuse victim and the Pollyanna, the actress and the authentic. Whatever the truth, I know I started moving away from the social and into the solitary that year. My desire for something real from God grew, and I even helped form a Bible study, kind of shocking myself. Something was definitely up in my soul, and it wasn't happy freshman year.

IF YOU DON'T COUNT MY HEART

When I finished my year-long tour, college started within weeks. I wasn't ready. Instead, I asked to go live with my dad's mother, now a widow in Colorado who needed companionship and care. Her health at 85 was a bit precarious; living alone was becoming less an option. There was talk of a nursing home in her future and after my year of visiting institutions of all kinds, that thought roused righteous indignation in me. I didn't even want to be a nurse anymore, and I surely didn't want my grandmother in a nursing home! Maybe I thought singing songs and talking about progress couldn't change the world, but I was pretty sure my living with Grandma could change hers'. My one broken wing was about to be joined by a second.

In her home, I experienced more of the pain and ambivalence that seemed to follow me everywhere. On the good side, my faith-life deepened; I had quiet spaces to think and feel after the headlong rush of a year in the spotlight. I spent time in Bible study, prayer, and

80

contemplation. I took long bike rides in the mountains, emulated my grandma's bird-like eating habits, and enjoyed a physical health that I never had before. We worked together in her gardens, and she cooked, while I did the cleanup, took her to medical appointments, and completed a correspondence course in college literature. Toward the end, I had a Christian guy profess his love to me, and although I was uncertain of us, it felt like something good was happening. My time in Colorado culminated in my baptism at age 21. I had been christened as a baby, sprinkled as a child, but desired to be immersed as an adult. If anyone should have been permanently washed, it was me!

But a long fall wound its poisonous way like a snake through my six months with Grandma. It started with her unholy charge that I was a harlot after she saw a guy kiss me goodnight at the front door, and ended with her devastating accusation that I had stolen from her: first her social security check (which I searched for and found), then her 50th anniversary diamond ring (which didn't show up until my uncle and aunt found it months later, wrapped in bits of plastic and string, hidden in a buffet drawer).

Living in the shadow of a maximum-security prison had made Grandma paranoid. This tendency, combined with early dementia and the obvious trials of living with a 20-year-old insensitive to the generations between us did us in.

I left the house in tears the day she accused me of stealing her ring, knowing that for both our sakes, I couldn't go back. Once again, I experienced home and family as an unsafe place and my hopes of saving the day were crushed. I loved my grandmother, just as most children do, yet it seemed like my love only hurt her. Another layer of pain and uncertainty settled into my heart. *This is all my fault. I've failed again. I have loved God here and all I have to show for it is a mess. What is wrong with me?*

The car ride home to Texas was almost unbearable. We sat together in the backseat, me in a cesspool of failure, accusation, and the knowledge that *because of me* she was likely going to end up in a nursing home. She was so angry she wanted to spit. She had to leave her home, her independence, her friends. It was supposed to be the other way around. I was supposed to save her from that fate! Instead, she was being taken out of her home to live with my parents, an arrangement that lasted about six months before she was moved again, unwillingly, to a nursing home where she died a few years later. I returned to college studies, woefully wishing I would have gone there six months earlier.

During my sophomore, junior, and senior years at Texas Tech, I was quite a different person. Subdued, serious, deeper. The guy who professed his love in Colorado withdrew it after the accusations of my grandmother became known to him. I felt accused all over again and rejected as flawed. To boot, my abuser was now on campus, having transferred from another university. I screwed up the unsanctified energy to treat him normally, even as I always had. To show the smile and hide the pain. Yes, I was glad to be back, but I had more scars to hide.

One scar tough to ignore was the injury I had sustained the previous January while skiing with friends in Colorado. I would find myself literally falling (no metaphor, here) during aerobics, going down steps, playing softball. My knee would swell and hurt, and then return to normal until the next time I moved just so and collapsed.

I had twisted my knee on a downhill run at Vail; my bindings froze, and my ski didn't pop off. Of course, I was trying to keep up with friends much better than I, trying to impress when I should have just gone to the bunny hill. My goggles fogged and I lost my friends anyway. And then I fell, blinded by falling snow. My immediate sensation was nausea, not pain. So, I got through it and skied the rest of the way down the mountain. Asking for help was one of my firm 'no-no's, and I would have been mortified to call for the ski patrol to carry me down, let alone go to a *doctor*. That was for imperfect people; the needy; the broken. I was so committed to never showing pain that I literally skied down a mountain in Colorado with a torn ACL. A person in our party looked at my swollen knee that night but, knowing I had skied after the injury, surmised I had a sprain.

Finally, months later after yet another sudden fall, I saw a doctor who said there was one sure way to test whether I had a sprain or a tear – to extract fluid from under the kneecap and check for blood. This he proceeded to do, and the pain was excruciating. I've borne children, and I'm pretty sure it didn't hurt that bad. Of course, after childbirth you have something wonderful to show for it. In this case, the only result was bloody synovial fluid, arthroscopy to expose the extent of the tear (complete), and surgery to replace a now atrophied ACL and remove the medial meniscus.

There are some stories in your life that tend to instruct you later, to reveal to a more mature you who *you used to be* as a child and young person. This is one of those stories. If I ever wonder whether I was a normal kid, I just think of skiing down that mountain with a torn ACL. It was a metaphor for my life.

THE DISTANCE DANCE

Recovery that summer was actually fun, as strange as that might sound. I worked off campus in the optometric practice of a family friend, and there I met his roommate, a fourth-year med student on his way to becoming a family-practice doctor. He came to visit me in the "horsepital" as he always called it, and we began dating. I had become involved in a big charismatic church in Lubbock, attending their college fellowship nights, studying, learning, growing again in my faith that had been so often tattered. He was involved in a small Baptist church with high mistrust for the charismatic. Plus, he had a close female friend at church whom I was pretty certain, with women's intuition (or just very good radar), wanted to marry him.

The distance dance ensued. His busy residency; my desire for closeness alternating with keeping the distance between us proportional: his trust of the scientific, even in faith; my foray into the charismatic spiritual realm. His tennis playing with "the other girl" from church; my recuperation from knee surgery. My feeling like a trophy girlfriend (I needed to look right); his insistence that no woman would mess with his manners, clothing choices, or faith practice (he needed to be himself). It literally fell apart one afternoon after we had dated about a year. He carved out a few hours for me one afternoon, then promptly fell asleep while we were kissing. It was too much distance, and I couldn't face a lifetime of it. Several years later, we were both married: he to the tennis partner, I to a young man from my college fellowship.

The fact that Art had asked me out while I was dating the doctor was actually a factor in the breakup. Another young man's interest, and the way he told me he had been praying about me, caught my attention. My other relationship seemed like a sham, emotionally void, while my early conversations with Art were alive spiritually, mentally, and physically. While the doctor attracted the logical side of me – he was kind, spiritual, smart and had a good professional life ahead – Art attracted the creative, passionate me. After our first date, I wrote in my journal that the conversation felt like fresh water flowing through my life. He was curious about everything I thought and believed, and quickly found a place in my heart. His faith was overtly strong; his gifts in music and readiness to share his faith attractive. Plus, he was handsome, sporting a beard, a guitar, and a ready smile. We got serious pretty fast, and although we attended the same college fellowship, I also began attending his Baptist church on a regular basis.

Sometimes I look back on those years and wonder how something that began so sweetly could disintegrate into such pathos, but it did. Maybe all it takes is two very broken young people who don't really know they are broken and perfect circumstances.

My parents saw it; in fact, they were party to it during our courtship as he took them to task over their beliefs and made himself unwelcome in our home. He once went on a camping trip with us and my Dad actually stopped the car and ordered him to get out. I felt caught, just like I had years ago when Mom made me say *the prayer*. I gritted my teeth, apologizing to all parties for something I hadn't done, and tried to keep the peace. At one point, my Dad said he didn't want to come to the wedding, and I begged until he recanted.

It was a mess with my family, and our personal relationship was getting messier too. I broke up with him, only to come back into relationship when he threatened suicide. The distance dance was on. We had fights. He hit car doors and walls, and I wondered when a fist would come my way. At one point in our engagement, he forced me to tell him about every physical encounter I had ever had, even though I was still a virgin due to God's grace and my own fear of sexuality. It wasn't enough that I sketched the big picture (including details of my abuse, which he already knew about), he became obsessed with knowing every detail, claiming it was a spiritual issue. I finally broke down but felt violated. Nauseated. Forced into vulnerability that hurt. It was like being forced to say *the prayer* all over again.

There was also push-pull to our physical relationship, even though there was no sex. He would move in closer and closer, then break away in guilt and anger, sometimes accusing me of tempting him, sometimes angry with himself for days. It was like a roller coaster – pulled closer, found desirable, pushed away, found guilty or left confused on the other end of his self-recrimination. Where I had nicely managed my freshman year, partying until 2 a.m., then getting up for 7 a.m. classes, I was now run ragged as he kept me up until all hours of the night, talking *at* me, not to me, about the latest thing he was upset about. I would finally simply give in, apologize for whatever the problem seemed to be, hoping I could word the apology well enough to convince him, and return, whipped, to my dorm room for some rest. This was a pattern I carried into our marriage and beyond, just letting him win for the sake of peace.

I was a resident assistant that year too, adding not only to my workload, but also to the risk of exposure as an entire group of people watched me for leadership. My hall got excited about decorating for Halloween, and I paid for it with Art, who thought Halloween was satanic. I counselled a young woman who came to me pregnant and scared. We talked her through the options, including adoption, one I urged her to consider. But it wasn't enough for Art, and to please him we met with the couple where he hounded them about repentance and salvation. Relationships were cut off, and I felt the "caughtness," the dreaded ambivalence of the war that I couldn't win. I stuffed it down and marched on toward the altar. After all, that is where you lay yourself down as a sacrifice, right? And so, despite all that was wrong, we married during the last half of my senior year.

The hook that landed me in pain so many times before had landed me again. My need to be loved. Art was so passionate. He wanted to know everything about me; he wanted to die if I wanted out. I felt so important, like the center of his world. This was a different kind of abuse, an obsession, not readily apparent to casual observers, but it began to control my every move. What I wore suddenly needed to please Art. What I said and thought and did and spent needed to pass his high bar. My friendships were cut off if he didn't approve, and he didn't approve of most of them, only tolerating my family – considered over-the-top religious folk in my small community. My past needed to be laid bare before him, and my purity needed to be beyond reproach. Over and over, I needed to prove that I trusted him, loved him, would follow his lead. I endured all the dysfunction for the moments where I felt treasured, loved, pursued, protected. It all happened under the banner of faith, and I believed that with faith, everything would turn out okay.

What I missed during all the time I spent spinning the tale I wanted others to see was that my heart was unguarded. *Awkward.* I was highly self-protective, but no one was protecting my innermost being. I had good intentions and tried to be a good person, but was categorically dishonest, sacrificing myself and my integrity to make others comfortable. Until you can see that good intentions aren't the same as integrity, and that you can't win your way to glory by your own efforts at being nice, "beautifully broken" sounds like an oxymoron.

Proverbs 4:23 teaches us that the very water of life flows from our heart and that it's part of our God-given responsibility to protect those springs. It took me forever to get that. I was busy hiding from truth and trying to find life by my own wits. The abuse, which had never been my fault, was now twisted up in decisions for which I was responsible. Pain and perfectionism and posing were driving my life, leading to decisions which made me less and less safe.

To the outside world, casual friends, church friends, I probably looked like I was doing great, maybe even successful, *if you don't count my heart.*

Chapter 6: Why Did I Get Hurt? Is This My Fault?
QUESTIONS FOR REFLECTION

Question: List an experience you had that taught you what freedom might feel like. Now contrast it to what you think freedom in Christ is. How are they similar? Different?

Question: As an adult, you probably know more about what makes a home relationally safe, but as a child you tend to think whatever you live is "normal." What makes a home truly safe, and how do you rank the different situations you've lived in?

Question: Think back over an abuse or trauma that happened in your young life; do you remember feeling like it was your fault and that something was wrong with you? Why?

Question: Do you have a story from childhood that looms large as a metaphor for your life after childhood? What is the story and what metaphor?

Question: I experienced a distance dance in my significant relationships that had to do with fear of being close. I pursued those I couldn't get too close to for a variety of reasons – yet I was desperate for love. Think about your own history with significant relationships, what kinds of patterns have you used to stay "safe" yet get love or feel significant?

Action: Buy yourself a notebook or journal if you don't already have one. Begin a page called "how I see myself," and list every metaphor you can think of that either silently or loudly echoes inside you. Begin another page with the words, "I believe life is…" and fill in the blank. (Examples from my life: I saw myself as the cartoon character, Pigpen, a little cloud following me everywhere I went. I believe life is serious, but others believe life is fun, life is a game, life is a circus, etc.) How do these metaphors and beliefs show up in your life and relationships?

Been chasing after dreams so long
But they were only mine
Feels like I've run a million miles
Always a step behind
And there's always been this longing
Something empty in my soul
And I've tried the right, I've tried the wrong
To get around this hole, but

I fell in and I fell down
'Til falling seemed to be
The thing that best defined me
But going down
Was where I found
My faith in something bigger
Than all that I could be
And falling's just the other side
Of longing to be free, yeah
I found Jesus in the black hole,
He was falling beside me.

And we were falling, falling, falling,
Then He caught my hand
And suddenly falling
Was just flying –
Falling was just flying
With Him holding on to me

February 2005

Chapter 7
Where are You, God? Why do I Keep Falling?

Early in my marriage to Art, we went out for a jog. I said something he didn't like, and in a flash, he shoved me down. I was no fool, and I knew that his own father had physically abused his mother; it was part of his traumatized childhood. Although he was completely aghast at what he had done and begged forgiveness, it changed me. I forgave, but I couldn't forget. Between the car door bashing, the fist into the wall, the shove, and the late-night verbal bullying, I got the message: Art couldn't handle any difference, any disagreement between us. *I better not use my voice unless I want to lose myself.*

The truth was, either way I lost myself, whoever that girl might have been.

It all happens slowly, the shutdown of a human soul. If you're already schooled to not feel what you feel, you just batten down that hatch after each new storm, fearful to open it again, because, like Pandora's box, turning those feelings loose would turn the world upside-down again. You go into denial. It is a way of dying to self, but it is not God's way.

My faith got a terminal illness during my six-year marriage to Art, or at least my desire to pursue God did. I still believed in God, but I was at a total and complete loss to understand what relationship with him should look like. That concept of freedom in Christ was a riddle, and I was beginning to think it was a riddle that couldn't have resolution.

Art asked me one day, five-and-a-half years in, where I would rank our marriage on a scale of one to 10. He quickly gave it a nine, probably hoping I would do the same. I daringly gave it a three or four, wondering how I would pay for my answer. At that point, he was kind of humbled, having lost several jobs, and working 60- or 70-hour weeks at a physically demanding position. He simply listened, unbelieving, but he never saw himself as the problem. Even when we went to counselling, I was the one who took the blame for the tension between us and he let me. I was afraid, even in front of a counsellor, to speak the truth about what I experienced, what I felt, what I endured.

People kept asking us when we were going to start a family. We were nearing 30 and it seemed the logical next step, but I was honest enough to admit (to myself anyway) that I didn't want to have children with him. For the first time in my life, I was considering suicide. I think my own hatred of conflict fused with his controlling behavior left me feeling it was the only way I'd ever escape. It was literally a shock to me – I had never understood why people wanted to die by their own hand. Despite the scary feelings, on some level they woke me up. I gained Art's agreement to go to a reunion of friends from my year of travel; the first time in our marriage I think we'd been apart. Somewhere during that week, in the space and silence, the idea began pounding me, *Amy, it's not that you want to die, it's that you want to live, and you're not!* It was as if, by opening the door to marriage with Art, I had closed the door to everything else life might offer.

I came home, knowing that things had to change. I began to exercise, lose weight, pursue the musical gifts that had died during my relationship with Art, and for the first time since college graduation, go after a real job. Music was a passionate love of mine from childhood, but somehow with Art it became a competition to prove who was right, who was better. I gave up; there just wasn't room for both of us. The same was true of my career. I had a bachelor's in journalism while he had a certificate from a community college. But any job I took had to be less important than his own so he wouldn't feel threatened. I auditioned for a band and began writing music again. I applied for several career-oriented jobs and landed one. But I was an accident just waiting to happen.

Maybe six months after I ranked our marriage at a three or four, he finally asked again where I was with regard to our marriage. When I hedged, he simply said, "Well, if you want to divorce me, I wish you'd get on with it because I've found someone new."

Boom. Obsession over. Thoughts of suicide unnecessary. The lion seemed suddenly toothless, and I wasn't going to wait around to see if those teeth grew back. I could live, and I was determined that, this time, I would find my way without God who seemed to just taunt me with perfection I could never reach. In my own words, as I announced the separation and plans for divorce to a family member I said, "I'm taking a sabbatical from God."

I was plagued by second thoughts after we separated. I had moved out, leaving him our home, and just taking a few pieces of furniture. I was ready to take the hits, to give him the savings and the house. I knew God hated divorce, and I didn't want to betray or anger God, I just wanted out of this terrible marriage. I wanted a sabbatical from God, not his abandonment; relief from what I didn't understand, not rejection. Unfortunately, all I knew of freedom boiled down to my freshman year in college: Doing what I wanted instead of what someone else wanted. I lacked a lot of maturity; emotional health that couldn't be gained by living the way I had been living.

Art soon wanted out of the financial burden of the house, and when the condo I was living in sold, I moved back to the house, assuming responsibility that would become mine in the divorce.

He came by one day asking to talk, and in the space of a few hours, recounted, one-by-one, every time he had punched me emotionally or spiritually; the ways his behavior had wrecked so many friendships and family relationships; the times he had frightened me with his temper. It shocked me that he remembered it all, as he had never taken responsibility for anything that hurt our relationship, save the shoving incident. It was as if a veil had been pulled back and he saw clearly all the behaviors that led us to this day. He confessed them and didn't try to bully me back into relationship as he would have previously. I thought, "He's really different."

I lay in bed that night, pondering what to do. In the end, I didn't trust him. If he actually knew those things were hurting me across the more than seven years we had known each other, why hadn't he done anything about it? Why had he kept hurting me emotionally and spiritually? Why had he let me absorb the blame in front of our counsellor, the financial weight of bills and now our home during separation?

I was so afraid to be snared in his trap again. Honestly, I didn't yet see how my early trauma and hatred of conflict played any part in the collapse of our marriage. I said nothing to him of my misgivings and we were quietly divorced as he prepared to wed again, and I continued the sabbatical I had started a few months before.

THE BLACK HOLE

The set up for a fall is often long. Yes, I had fallen before. Partially because of what had happened to me before age 21, I was trying to adult with two broken wings. And of course, I had made mistakes; I had missed the mark just like every human being does. But I had desired good for others, and I had desired to *be* good. Mistakenly, I thought my passive goodness would overcome evil. In a theologically unsound way, I was trying to live out Paul's advice to Christians, "overcome evil with good (Romans 12:21)." I was being "good" out of fear, out of woundedness, out of desire to control others' impressions. Trust of God was absent.

Leading up to the separation from Art, something in me was changing. I could see all my being good had only gotten me here – in a dangerous and soul-killing marriage to a man who seemed more like Judas Iscariot than Jesus Christ. I stopped listening to Christian music as had been my habit for a decade and tuned the radio to songs that made me think of all I seemed to be missing. I started doing some inner work around co-dependency and read some books that introduced new ideas about freedom from rules and people. That sounded good.

I began to ask questions about just what kind of a god God was. Where had he been when I needed rescue as a child? Why had those who purported themselves Christians hurt me, abandoned me in my early abuse, and been so cruel in my young adulthood?

I stopped trying so hard to be good and found myself entertaining new temptations. God had failed me it seemed, and now I would find life on my own.

As a child and youth, I had always prayed for wisdom and faithfulness, even in the midst of my abuse. Now, on the cusp of my 30th birthday, I felt those prayers dead. I began to walk away from my marriage and my God, slowly, in my head. Particularly, I began to consider men other than Art. This was something I had simply never struggled with, and between my hungry heart and naïve ways of thinking, the downhill slide was dizzying. I had practiced a moral lifestyle for 30 years, but it took only one year to undo it all.

I had a long commute that year and found myself checking out every man in every car. And sometimes they were looking at me too. There are two things I know now: One, there are an awful lot of lonely people out there looking for a fix. If sex is your fix, you'll find it almost as soon as you start to look. Two, sex outside of marriage can't fix your empty heart, but it can sure wreck your life.

God says that when you harden your heart against the truth, he'll let you walk away; he'll turn you over to the darkness of your own thinking. I think it's not because he *doesn't* love you, it's *because he does*. God hopes when you taste that fruit, maybe you won't like it. But God also knows that we are wired by the fall to try hard to validate our own thinking. Mine was a long, hard fall, set in motion by emptiness and loss, abandonment, and betrayal. But then, there was choice. My choice. My hand to the fruit of the knowledge of good and evil, and then my hand to my mouth, trying to *taste and see that the world was good*. Then there were years, more than a decade of precious years, that I tried to validate my choices in order to live with myself.

It started innocently enough, a new communications job without that long commute. I deeply admired my new boss, and unbeknownst to him, had watched him with his pre-teen daughters one day at a restaurant before I was hired. I thought him remarkable to give time and attention to them.

It seemed the sign of a good father, a good man. I didn't know that they lived in another state and had only come for a brief visit. Then, Art and I separated, and I moved to the condo. One day, my boss casually mentioned that his wife wanted a divorce. There was a click and no pause. *Maybe this was the man for me.* I watched as he began an affair with another woman. There was another click and no pause, *I have to fight for him if I want him.*

And so, I began a campaign to convince him we made a good team. A good dating team, a good working team. He was 13 years older, but I told him it didn't matter. He listened, but didn't buy in, saying he didn't believe in mixing work with romance. Still, he went with the other woman to a business convention we were all part of, and in my growing contempt toward being a "good girl," I got drunk and threw away integrity with a man I barely knew. At the time it seemed I was drawing a line in the sand. I was going forward to divorce, with or without the man I loved, and definitely without what remained of the moral compass of my youth and the blessing of God. How little did I know the cost of those decisions, bitter and defiant. Now, the way was thoroughly paved for what would soon follow.

Months later, my boss and I found ourselves alone in a hotel room one night, having completed the first day of a conference we were hosting. One kiss led to another, and another, and within moments, the idea of starting out with dating was far, far behind us. Ambivalence reigned. I was ashamed; I was shameless. My divorce would soon be final and I thought his would be too. Wrong.

Friday night we attended a party to mark the end of the successful conference. In high spirits, we drank and danced, keeping hidden what had happened the night before. Then we drove home and spent the night together. I came home Saturday morning and slept most of the day, content with our plan to see each other Sunday.

I woke up Saturday night nauseated and threw up for the next 40 hours. I called him Sunday morning and told him I was too sick to keep our plans, then drew a cold bath to soak in. I was burning up and throwing up, and my only instincts were to keep drinking the grape juice I had to go downstairs to the refrigerator to get, then take yet another cold bath.

Sunday came and went, and I was not attuned to the passing of time. Monday morning when I didn't show up for work and didn't answer the phone, he came to the condo after calling the police. When the doorbell rang, I somehow stumbled down the stairs and opened the door, and the look on his face was one of disbelief. Later, he told me I was green, but that day, he just suggested he take me to the hospital. I agreed and grabbed a plastic bag to catch whatever was left in my stomach.

How is it that the man who saves your life is also the man with whom you have become an adulterer? How is it that the God from whom you have taken a sabbatical arranges for a visiting British doctor in the ER who takes one look – *literally one look* at you, and says, "I think she might have toxic shock, get her started on fluids and antibiotics." How is it, when they wheel you into the CT scan room just a few minutes later and note your vital organs have begun to shut down, you live on? How is it that you can be so close to death and not really comprehend it?

Three decades have passed and I still ponder these things. They shook me to the core, and it was months before I felt normal again. I said to my boss who both saved me and helped me wreck myself, "I don't know if you believe in Jesus, but I do, and if I am to die, I want you to believe too." To which he replied, "How could I believe in a god who would take you from me?"

I still believed God had some kind of right to my faithfulness, even as I slowly replaced him with another god. The fall was long and hard, and the healing is still not complete.

It was my mother who came to nurse me back to health. Lying in the hospital, sicker than I knew, I remember saying, "It's strange to be 30 years old, in the ER, and the only thing you can say is, 'I want my mother!' She came, spending hours on the phone, in airports, and in cars to get to my side within 24 hours. I was 2,000 miles from home and it was no quick trip. She stayed two weeks, a private-duty nurse in her element and a mother to the rescue of a daughter who needed her. She helped me follow doctor's orders after I was released, fixed whatever food sounded good (mostly sliced veggies) so I could regain strength. I was greatly weakened by the infection, although thankfully had no permanent damage to organs, fingers, or toes.

Mom was honest, her love was obvious. And I was honest with her. I said, "Don't ask if you don't really want to know the answer, because I will tell you the truth." The walls between us came down, often with her in tears, hearing what she didn't want to. But she didn't reject me or go home angry to nurse her wounds. It was probably my first experience of true freedom and *agape* love, speaking the truth while knowing that I wasn't going to be abandoned for making choices that didn't please her. Even at the precipice of the black hole, God was using circumstances to teach me things I would never forget: Like what love actually feels like when conflict is present and how being honest about your flaws and faults with someone who loves you is hard, but cleansing.

The obvious irony of sleeping with a man and getting toxic shock syndrome, which the doctors could not explain by standard rationale, never escaped me. I should have quit the relationship, but I didn't. I had invested everything in a new moral code, now I had to justify my choices to live with myself. I would have married him then, but we were both still married to others and he wasn't asking anyway.

Ours was a relationship with no strings. I had given everything without asking anything.

LONG SET UP, LONG FALL

Months into our relationship, he told me more about his own belief system one day as we took a walk. He applied one of his favorite sayings, "We seek pain for the gift that it holds," to circumstances such as starvation, seeing it as a type of karma that would help people become ready for a reincarnated life. I didn't understand the idea of *seeking* pain, it seemed to find me of its own accord. I was pretty certain it found innocent people on the other side of the world too; they didn't need to draw it to themselves. It seemed to me a view that lacked compassion, though I wouldn't have wanted to cause conflict between us by saying that. As it came back to me over the years, it dawned on me that I had, indeed, sought pain – just not in the way he spoke of.

I found out that when he went home to his family almost 800 miles away, he still functioned as married. With his talk of divorce, I had assumed their separation in distance was a marital separation. I felt it as a betrayal, yet she was the one betrayed. It went to the core of my being, where that terrible ambivalence lived, with pain and anger twisted up in love and longing. What we found acceptable in relationship was very different, and what I saw as a clean-cut divorce started feeling more like a double-timing affair. One that dragged on several years and would eventually result in his children blaming me for the divorce between their parents.

I was ready to let him go, telling him that if there was *anyone else* he should be with, it was her. But he said he wanted out of his marriage and would make that clear when he went home. There was a distance dance alright, and the steps were getting more and more costly.

An all-too-familiar obsessive quality characterized our relationship, and while it made me feel loved, its' intensity was draining. He became entangled in yet another affair when I asked for a break as my divorce from Art approached. I couldn't process divorce and us at the same time. His affair shocked and hurt me, and any thinking I wanted to do about my own life was suddenly overshadowed by panic. We had to work together, and, although I absolutely loved my job, the office suddenly felt as unsafe as the homes I had lived in. All the reasons why work and romance don't mix suddenly made a lot more sense.

If you had tried to tell me the year before I would find myself in this kind of situation, I would have laughed in your face. I still knew the difference between right and wrong, but my choices and actions seemed driven by something bigger than my beliefs. As I look back, I believe I was living out what psychologists call *reenactment* – the idea that repeating the trauma of childhood is an attempt to get a better outcome. I can also see that I was vulnerable to repeating trauma because I lacked honesty and insight about my early life. It was like trying to drive with a flat tire. I kept on going, but the ride was bumpy and there was more and more damage as I pretended reality away.

My own divorce complete, I longed for our relationship again. I wanted him to erase all the pain and tell me he loved me. But I was sidelined, watching him with someone else again. Still, with my long history of hiding pain, I could take it; I could show up to work, swallow the bile and absorb the almost visceral hits to my insides. This is a scene that repeated many times in my life: observe what is hurting me without reacting on the outside. Deep ambivalence, deeper *MO*: smile on, don't let anyone see the pain. Although I didn't know it at the time, the proverb, "One who is full loathes honey from the comb, but to the hungry even what is bitter tastes sweet (Proverbs 27:7 NIV) was proving true. I was famished for something real and willing to consume even what was bitter. The damage I was doing to myself was going to leak someday.

In the end, we came back together, although there certainly was no victory party. We lost the company due to a business partner who stole money. I pursued him through the financial and psychic pain of a loss that impacted both of us, never asking for anything, just giving, spinning, hoping, caring, justifying. I thought I was being mature. That's how twisted my thinking was. I knew absolutely nothing about boundaries, and little about enabling. It's a sad but powerful truth that, as adults, we teach others how to treat us. I just didn't know what I didn't know.

I was responsible for a home of my own, and the mortgage and bills kept coming. I couldn't make ends meet but didn't ask for help. A downturn in the economy made the house impossible to sell, but eventually the bank accepted the deed in lieu of foreclosure. It was another hard loss in the midst of so many others. Still, with him in my life, I felt like I could do anything.

It would be irresponsible to not acknowledge the good in him – the things that attracted me in the first place. I have learned that when we classify a relationship or experience as all bad, we toss it out completely, preventing us from being able to learn from what was good and helpful. This man, who became my husband of 10 years and father to my girls, was really good in business relationships. He had a master's degree in teaching, and it showed up in his ability to unpack business concepts and make people want to reach for more. He was broadminded and free thinking and that was attractive to me, emerging from a controlling and legalistic marriage. He loved the land and the outdoors, and we enjoyed walks and hiking and an occasional vacation to a beautiful destination. He especially loved working with wood, and the smell of a shop with fire in the stove took me back to my childhood when I experienced my grandfather's workshop.

I don't know if he told me all his secrets, but I bear enough of them to know he had his own stories of pain, events he handled very differently than I did mine. That's really no surprise of course, but I was naïve enough to think others were like me, and it was an error, time after time, that caused me to fall into unsafe relationships. He didn't try to hide the affairs he had over the course of his lifetime or other stories of causing pain too, and while I can tell how that impacted my life, the stories of how he wounded others are his to process and tell, and I pray he will someday. Back then, I assured myself those were in the past. Now he was a different man.

The truth is it was I who became a different woman. Just like I learned in my first marriage to silence my voice, this relationship taught me to swallow my sense of right and wrong. The drive to not be left alone was powerful, so I stayed connected even when it hurt. Traumatic injuries can make you do that. Your recoil reflex gets broken. You put your hand on a hot stove and just leave it there, the ambivalence of pain and need for warmth colliding in your soul. According to James 1:5-8, being double-minded makes you unstable – in *all* your ways. In that condition, James says, don't even ask God for wisdom because you're being driven by wind and waves and will doubt whatever God might say. How true that was for me.

When we married, we wrote our own vows of course. One of his statements to me was, "I will be true to your charms." *What does that even mean?* I wondered, but I hated conflict and so said nothing. *I guess as long as I am charming, he will be true to me*, I thought.

Of course, I *intended* to be charming.

I told him when we married that I would not tolerate infidelity, and I meant it. I assumed someday he would tell the children of his previous marriage that he had been unfaithful to their mother for years, and that the divorce was inevitable. They both wanted it, and not because of me. Not only was he never honest with them about his part in the divorce, there was also friction between us as I tried to advocate for his presence in his daughters' lives. I thought he should be near them, so even though we were considering starting a business somewhere else, I urged him to put down roots close to them. It took me further from my extended family but seemed the right thing to do.

His girls were in their teen years, and I wanted him to help them learn to drive. After a lot of pleading on my part, and an accident for his oldest, he finally told me, "Butt out, I don't tell you how to run your family." Since I had no children, what he was really saying was, *you have no part in my daughter's lives.* It was a zinger intended to shut me up, and it did. After all, I had accepted the relationship without strings, and had never asked for a voice. Still, one of the biggest tragedies of our relationship for me was the way my stepdaughters felt toward me. I could understand it, because they blamed me for the divorce and subsequent pain in their lives, but I grieved it. It was something I never saw coming, and again I witnessed my power to hurt others, even when it was far from my intention.

The truth is, even if his marriage was doomed by affairs, I didn't have to be one of them…but I was, and a lot of innocent people got hurt, most of all our children.

THE TRUTH LEAKS

A year and two months after we married, we had our first child together, a daughter, and two and a half years later, another daughter. We built several businesses, me always playing a role in our success, sometimes large, sometimes small. I was losing my charm though, between the rigors of parenting two toddlers at age 40 and trying to keep the plates spinning. He had told me before we married, "Okay, we can have babies, but we have to do it before I'm 50, and you have to raise them. I won't be involved until they are older."

As an older Mom, an amnio was suggested by my OBGYN, but I didn't want that. I reasoned the only thing it could accomplish was a more stressful pregnancy if there was a hint of anything wrong. My husband didn't agree, and it became clear that if there was something wrong, I would be expected to undergo abortion. I often think back about the moment that was said – that was the moment I should have run as far away as I could get, but I carried on, frightened of conflict, what looked like my weakness, and losing this connection for which I had sacrificed so much.

It was hard being so alone in parenting. I had waited to be a mom until I was 36. Now, not only did I have a partner unwilling to share the load except when absolutely necessary, I had no one to share the joys of those years with. As any single parent can tell you, it's painful to not be able to have someone with whom to witness the joys and talk over the challenges.

I always wanted to be a stay-at-home mom and had told him that the very first time we had lunch together almost eight years before. He hadn't understood it then, and he didn't now. So, I toggled between jobs, trying to mother and trying to be the independent woman he had married. If I ever left the babies with him, I came home to find them crying in a corner, or unattended while he read his latest business tome. Once he set our toddler at the top of the front porch while he packed the car for a trip. She fell down three concrete steps. It wasn't so much that it happened; I could forgive an accident if he had shown the least concern, but in a fit of impatience and contempt for my caution, he took off on the trip without me. I called the doctor.

Being in a position of responsibility for little lives was one of the best things that ever happened to me. It brought out the better me, but my emptiness was also catching up, and my spinning becoming a slow twirl. The cracks were about to show, the leaking begin.

When the kids were three and five, he suggested I look for work. I had left my last communications job under difficult circumstances just before we married, and still had a terrible taste in my mouth. But I wanted to please him, and we needed the money, so I applied for a huge job and astonishingly, walked out with it after my first interview. I was just what they were looking for. Not.

I was good at my job. I had a great work ethic and loved my responsibilities, but I've never been very snobbish. It was a non-profit in an elite sector of the economy, and it wasn't long before the head of the organization, who hadn't wanted my boss to hire me anyway, wanted me gone. I was down-to-earth, friendly, and more than a little naïve, despite the road I had walked. Politics at work always confused me, then and now. I'm not political or cagey. My boss was caught; she liked me, but my left-handed, right-brained creative style was different from her logical, linear approach. My way of doing things was hard for her to understand.

One thing at my job that I wasn't skilled at was managing a budget. I was creative and spontaneous, but budgeting and bill paying required constancy. Maintenance never seemed as important as action to my highly creative and slightly ADD brain.

During my tenure, massive airplanes full of innocent people crashed into the twin towers in New York City and the Pentagon, and another went down on its way toward the White House. I remember watching the second tower crash before running, terrified, to pick my kindergartner. The world went crazy. People avoided big events like ours for months, and our revenue stream was immediately impacted. I was panicked and kept trying to hold onto money; my boss kept trying to get me to do business as usual, maintaining status quo, especially vendor relationships. And so, when a pink slip came my way, it came with kind words from her, and apologies. I could stay as long as it took to find another job. She believed in me; just didn't think I was a good fit.

I was mortified, humiliated. '*What is wrong with me?*' was the familiar and harsh tape that played. *I feel like falling is what defines my whole life.* I had been pink slipped at another communications job I really loved, and at almost 40, had no truly happy endings in my vocational life – the kind where you move up and on, satisfied that you've done well, in others' eyes as well as your own. I had encountered abuse, been abandoned by my parents when I needed them most, lost a marriage and a home and a relationship with my grandmother. A decade earlier, I had run from God, and now it felt like he had abandoned me. My goodness didn't matter, and no matter how hard I tried, how much I gave, it was never enough. My spinning wasn't working, and I was out of gas. The questions echoed around and around in my head, never coming to any answer but this: The only way out is to never try again. *Maybe I am a permanent loser. Maybe I will always end up ruining whatever I touch.*

Depression became my constant companion. The black hole felt more visceral than metaphoric, sucking the life out of me. I knew one of my husband's favorite sayings was "success is the only option," and I felt like a failure in his eyes. Before 9-11, he was on his way to success with one of the companies we had started, and here I was, an embarrassment to his success.

Failing in life, at work, and in relationship made me ask hard questions. Questions I had often avoided throughout my life by simply spinning faster, trying harder to please, ignoring the way I felt, and marching on. Questions I had no margin for as I fell, like *why can't I find peace, or success, or love? Does God hate me; has he abandoned me? Is God even real?*

The freedom I had longed for when my first marriage broke up had burned to ashes. I had set in motion a way of being in my new relationship, a no-strings-attached liaison based around the bedroom and the boardroom. Now, I was a 41-year-old unemployed woman, less confident than I had ever been. I had gained 20 pounds with each pregnancy, was tired all the time, depressed, and often just going through the motions. I felt used up and powerless.

I hated being needy, but I needed help and didn't know how to ask. I had never set a boundary in my life that was strong, secure, and unyielding to whatever someone else thought. I weeded out opinions of my own, preferring instead to draw out what others were thinking and feeling. My husband and I had a quiet relationship – no fights really because in our dynamic, there was really nothing to fight about. I pleased; he was fine with that. And I can't really blame him. I helped him become the way he was by never negotiating the relationship; I made my own bed and then decided it was really uncomfortable. I pulled a bait and switch on him, whereas he stayed true to his way of being throughout our relationship. I'm not saying that was right or good, only that I'm culpable for teaching people how to treat me.

This wasn't freedom. I had willingly ignored every sign along the way to this marriage, becoming a prisoner of my own free, but foolish will. Now, I felt like a reed in the wind, or a flickering candle. I could be blown down, or blown away, by the slightest puff. The good news for souls like mine was just a heartbeat away. I began to crumble. A sermon I heard while visiting family, left me, who never cried, weeping at the verse, "A bruised reed he will not break, and a smoldering wick he will not snuff out. In faithfulness he will bring forth justice; he will not falter or be discouraged till he establishes justice on earth (Isaiah 42:3-4)."

God would not break me or snuff out my life. He wanted justice, not revenge. I couldn't tell you what day it happened, but one moment I was falling into a black hole with no bottom, the next I had a vision that, even though I was falling, I wasn't alone. There was a friend beside me in the plummet, holding onto me. That friend knew how to fly downward at great speeds. And to that one, Jesus, falling was just flying.

THE GIFT OF CHILDREN

Children are a gift from God, and I think we don't always anticipate how that gift will show up. In my case, needing answers for their questions about God drove me back toward faith. Watching their joy reminded me of how I had started out too; before the abuse, full of joy and promise and questions I believed could be answered.

I wanted to be a great mom. To do things differently than my own mom, who never really seemed to enjoy children. I was driven to get help because I saw myself taking my anger and frustration with marriage out on our girls – and I knew it couldn't go on. The final straw came one day as my youngest was dallying around and I was trying to get her out the door to pre-school. In no uncertain terms, I told her to put on her shoes and she just looked at me and said, "Mommy, you're a bad mommy."

That should have been enough to make me cry, but I didn't cry. What popped out of my mouth feels unforgivable, even though I've asked her forgiveness several times over the years. "Well," I said, angrily, "maybe you're just a bad daughter!"

No. No. No. The shame of such words coming from my mouth burned worse than any shame I had endured. This was not the woman I was going to become. I had crossed a line, and by God's grace, I would never cross it again.

I went to a pastor-friend about that incident, so full of pain and regret, and he helped me by noting that my daughter was about the same age I had been when my abuse started. Her devil-may-care attitude always kind of shocked me. She was so different from her sister, two-and-a-half years older. Precocious was the word many people used of her, mouthy and loud, while my oldest was gentle, soft spoken, and wanted to please. My ah-ha that day was that my youngest triggered in me my own loss of carefree childhood, and that maybe, just maybe, she was the tough little angel God sent to prick my heart. I would pull up my big girl britches and try to become the mother they both deserved.

The downside, after giving my husband god-status for almost a decade, was that he was used to it. When I started my return toward God, having a few boundaries, and asking for things to be different, that pedestal tipped. I found the underbelly of his character, and things between us got far worse than I bargained for.

My depression took a toll on our household. I have many regrets for those years; they were some of the most difficult in my life. The dishes and laundry stacked up. There were piles and messes in every room it seemed. Life with little children is chaotic, and I get that, but I was not good at cleaning and organizing (think maintenance) on a perfect day – and there were no perfect days those years.

One day, a framed picture of the girls at ages one and three, dressed up like the angels they were, got knocked off the mantle and the glass shattered into our carpet. I felt shattered too, and for months, I could never pick up that mess. It just stayed like that, my better angels lying on the floor, and became a no-go zone.

The life I was living just couldn't go on. Maybe being apart would help us both figure out where we needed to change as individuals, and so I asked if we could separate for that purpose.

During the months prior, I had finally told a dear family member about my battle with depression. She knew of a chain of Christian counselling clinics around the country where a friend had received help and asked me to look into it. She made me promise that I would never think of taking my life, and if I did, that I would call her. That felt like love to me. Someone willing to enter the conflict with me, the pain, the collision of all my hopes and dreams with the reality I was living.

Ironically, about the same time, my childhood abuser wrote a letter asking my forgiveness. He had attempted to talk to me before, but in my commitment to pretending nothing was ever wrong, I had brushed him off. Now his own black hole made him reach out again. He was advised by a 12-step sponsor that he needed to make restitution as the next step in his own recovery. He offered financial help for any counselling I had need of to recover. Although I had already decided to go for help, the timing was important, and the one who damaged me in childhood became part of my healing.

Late on New Year's Eve, 2002, dreading another year before me, I called the closest Minirth-Meier Clinic (now called Meier Clinics). Ironically, or not in God's economy, the clinic was just 35 miles away. I never expected an answer, just wanted to leave a message. But the phones were forwarded to an on-call counsellor, and he did an intake on the spot, taking time away from a New Year's Party he was attending and ending with, "I think our three-week outpatient intensive would be right for you."

The new year came, and I began a new journey. Climbing out of the black hole was actually harder than falling into it had been, but I found the strength to face the journey from the one for whom falling was just flying.

Question: Has any truth you've tried to hide come leaking out despite your best efforts?

Question: If you, like I, have ever found yourself considering suicide, how much does wanting to die have to do with actually wanting to live and not feeling like you are?

Question: Have you ever taken a "sabbatical" from God? Why and what were the results?

Question: In what ways do you relate to my statement that, as adults, we bear some responsibility for teaching others how to treat us?

Question: What slippery slopes have you found seductive? What have you done to justify your actions? What have you done to stop them?

Action: Do you have a person in your life you can be completely honest with? In moving toward freedom from addiction, Twelve-Step groups ask participants to make "a fearless moral inventory," and admit the exact nature of their wrongs to God, themselves, and another human. In a similar way, the Bible says confession leads to healing (James 5:16). Do some reading on confession and find one step you can take toward healing.

You can walk all day and only see sand,
Baby, this ain't the Promised Land

2006

Chapter 8
Where is This Promised *"Promised Land"*?

As I exited the outpatient intensive at Minirth-Meier Clinic, two important things had happened. First, I heard anew about Satan, that power that had decimated Job's life, his family, his possessions, his friendships, his reputation, his health. The story that had so intrigued me as a child returned to me as an adult, broken and needy.

Satan had been allowed to take everything but Job's breath, and his wife told him he should give that up, curse God, and just die already. And why? Why had God allowed such devastation to overwhelm one so faithful? Because God knew Job's heart and he was willing to wager (*what, God, place a bet?*) that Job's love for him wasn't based on worldly or relational accomplishments. Satan whined, 'Foul! He only loves you because you protect him!' God said, 'No, I believe it's deeper than that.'

I didn't like the idea that God would even tolerate a visit with the devil, and I had very much put the notion of an evil force in our world behind me – no more than a childish fable about a man in red with pitchfork, or the rantings of a mother who sprinkled holy water and cast out demons lurking around every corner. But I also found that if I saw my life story through the Biblical teachings about evil, and there are *a lot* of them (see Chapter 2), I could better comprehend suffering. Not that I was righteous like Job, but that there was promise in my life. A promise Satan saw more clearly than I. I found a determination to live into *that* promise more than the lie I heard constantly: *I'm a permanent loser who will always end up ruining whatever I touch.*

This was the beginnings of a theology of evil, even though that's not what I called it. It helped me answer some profoundly troubling questions like *why do bad things happen?* A deeper appreciation flowed out of my own failure to be perfect. I began to understand that no human being was perfect, not my parents, not my abuser, and not the two men I had married out of my own woundedness. Even a perfect God couldn't force any of us to make good decisions, and in fact, God had set in motion long ago the free will that either led to evil or good. He was so committed to free will that he had endured thousands of years of being wounded himself by our sinful choices.

My new understanding also suggested that if evil were so committed to my destruction, God must have something for me to do. Maybe it was vocational, maybe it was something about my daughters, maybe it was something about his church. I didn't have a clue, but the thought kept me going through many dangers, toils, and snares. It was God's will, whatever it was, and I wanted it to be done.

The second big thing that happened was I was asked to plan a strategy for reentering my life outside of the IOP. What support systems would I need, what books would I read, and would I commit to pray over these needs? These weren't plans for flying, I could see that. These were plans for walking on, regrouping, relearning, finding out who I really was for the first time, not by looking at the abyss inside, but by conversation with God and safe others, and engagement with God's words once again.

I had a list with about ten things as I recall; the first was praying for a group of women who understood how to walk back from childhood sexual abuse. Another was to find a new church. Our current one had a sort of high church vibe with little relational or spiritual depth, which worked fine if you were running from God, but not very well if you were trying to come back. I discovered my hunger for truth, and I was going to buy it, whatever the cost (Proverbs 23:23). Another thing on the list was to approach my husband with the truth of what our lifestyle and history was doing to me – not to blame, but to enter conflict honestly, pulling out the collective pain beneath the carpet, talking truth about where we were, what and where we needed to grow, and what our girls needed. Another was to finish reading a book that had literally changed my life during the three weeks of the IOP, *The Wounded Heart*, by Dr. Dan Allender.

I left the program on a Friday night, and on Saturday asked my little girls if they'd like to try a new church the next day. My husband left town, getting away to our property up north as he often did on weekends. I had asked the girls before, and they had always been hesitant, so I promised to visit the church where our youngest attended pre-school. Surprisingly, they said yes, and one of my prayers was answered.

Somehow, I got the service times wrong and found myself at the visitor's counter with time to kill before the second service began. There in front of me was the answer to my primary need on that list, and maybe hundreds of prayers I had never articulated: a brochure, announcing that this church was bringing in Dan Allender and his seminar,

Learning to Love Your Story, in March. *What? How is this possible?* I flipped the brochure over, wondering who in the world would bring such a conference to a church like this, and saw the name of an organization I never knew existed. Not far, far away, but within miles of my home. *Open Hearts Ministry,* read the ministry name and logo above the return address.

I couldn't wait for Monday morning to make a call and find out who in the world they were. Then, I walked into the spacious worship center at a church just a few miles from our home, and the sermon began. A series on Christian sexual identity. *What? A church talking about sexual identity? Where have I landed, and is prayer really this powerful?*

Monday morning found me on the phone to *Open Hearts Ministry* as soon as I got the girls to school. The receptionist was out, but the executive director answered my call. He told me the ministry published curriculum and ran trainings as well as small groups for those recovering from all kinds of abuse – all around the world. Yes, there were groups in town, but the 12-week sessions were already underway for several weeks and were now closed due to the confidential nature of the ministry. However, he knew of a group 45 miles away that might still be open and would make a phone call and get back to me.

That's the story of how, on Friday, I walked out of an IOP praying, on Sunday found a church to which I would belong for the next decade, and on Tuesday, found myself in a group of women journeying toward recovery from spiritual, emotional, sexual, and physical abuse. Not just any group, run by any leader. The group steered by the wise and incredibly loving founder of the ministry, Sandy Burdick. A *spiritual cardiologist,* with the tools to examine and treat the most wounded heart; a woman of strength and purpose who was the answer to my prayer.

The executive director of the ministry and his wife became steadfast friends too, and within months I had another woman of great wisdom and grace in my life, Mary Bonham. She told me one day as she was praying for me God prompted her, "just be her friend." And over the two decades since, she has lived into that like none other. When I turned my ears toward God, he turned his toward me. "Draw near to me and I will draw near to you," he said (James 4:8).

IS THIS THE PROMISED LAND?

The beginnings of trust were established between God and me those few weeks. No stone had been left stacked in the barricade between me and the road to recovery. I had heard confession of and received restitution for my childhood abuse. The resources were there to attend three intensive weeks of counselling and group work as I examined my depression, my history, my relationships, and my beliefs. I had a new faith family at a church where there was depth to the preaching and teaching, and I had a group of women to help me understand how the dynamics of abuse were playing out into my broken life. I had answers to prayers.

"The desert is God's place," a renowned guest preacher said at church one day. "If you're in the desert, for God's sake, stop running and listen!"

And so, I stopped my running and spinning.

As much as I learned over the next few years, however, becoming still and listening for God, I still didn't know that recovery was only the slave leaving Egypt, not the priest entering the Promised Land. That place was still a long way off, although its mirage was ever before me. Before me there was only sand, and a lot of it.

Chapter 8: Where is This Promised *"Promised Land"?*
QUESTIONS FOR REFLECTION

Question: Do you have a "theology" of evil even if you don't call it that? What is it?

Question: What do you believe about prayer?

Question: Is there a difference between the kind of prayers I was encouraged to begin after the IOP and simply turning to God in a crisis or when I have a need? What?

Action: Find a place near home where you can walk in some sand – a playground, a beach, etc. Remind yourself how different it is walking or running or jumping in sand than on a road or path. Would you be willing to spend more time in the sand if you knew it was going to make you stronger?

Move in closer, it's okay
I know that you've been hurt
I know you don't feel safe, but
Move in closer to His heart anyway,
You've found the only One
who knows
The way out and the way in
And the way that you were made by Him
The way up and the way around
The way that evil tried to take you down
The way through hell and the way back home
And the way that it should be
If you'll look into His heart I know you'll see
He knows the way

October 2006

Chapter 9
Does God Really Have a Plan?
(Because This Seems Like Chaos!)

My husband and I had been separated for six months. The time had been hard, but good in many ways, for me at least. I took time to rest and read books that built me up spiritually. Although the timeline is lost to me now, sometime during this unsettled period, we attended a marriage class offered by one of our employees, and also saw a marriage counsellor.

For the separation, he had refused to move out and so I suggested that we rent an apartment and switch off parenting time, an arrangement called 'birdnesting,' which allowed the girls to stay home all the time while we were the ones shuffling back and forth. It seemed wise at the time, and as fair to the children as the circumstance of separation could be. I saw our youngest daily after kindergarten, and then he picked them both up after our 2nd grader finished the day on his weeks. We alternated weeks in our home, save Wednesday, when the girls stayed with me as I recall – it didn't seem good for me or them to be apart so much. I also tried to talk to them every evening by phone during the other days, something he seemed to find annoying.

The marriage class was painful in many ways, and I never felt a breakthrough in our relationship. He told me I was unforgiving, and I couldn't find the words then, but I know now that I was looking for a change in his heart, in his treatment of me. It never happened. He confessed once to having a cold heart, but instead of changing that, I saw his actions entrenching it. I didn't trust him. He wanted my forgiveness but wasn't willing to say how or why he'd harmed me or our relationship. He had promised me 'no more lies,' but now told me that when telling the truth makes life more painful, he would lie. He said, "I wish we could find an easier way," when I wished we could find a way to reconciliation, an integrity where both our voices mattered. I was now trying to negotiate a relationship that had never existed, and it didn't go over very well.

As part of my commitment returning from IOP, I made a list of issues I believed needed to be addressed before our relationship could experience healing. I presented it to him, then to our pastor when we went to him for counselling, then to the marriage counsellor to whom the pastor referred us. Our marital *MO* was no conflict. We'd swept our differences under the rug for eight years of marriage and 10 years of relationship. Sadly, neither my husband, the pastor, nor the counsellor would deal with the list. It was as if my voice meant nothing. After maybe eight sessions, I remember this Christian counsellor turning to my husband and saying, "I can't do anything more to help your marriage, but if you want to continue to meet with me, we could do that." I was dismissed, my list unvisited in a file folder in his desk drawer, while my husband was invited into a private relationship with our counsellor (who shortly after lost his license for inappropriate sexual behavior). What a mess. I wouldn't even believe it if it hadn't happened to me.

We came back together after six months, but it was a rocky path we were walking. I'm sure he wanted out, and I started hearing phone calls late in the night in the basement, where he would go down to talk. I saw evidence of flirtations and worse, he lied to me about a trip he was taking, and who he would see there. One time, he introduced me by his ex-wife's name to some business associates. It all began to paint a clearer picture of what we were up against.

I had changed; my faith was stronger and my desire to see our marriage change was stronger too. I had always believed the husband set the agenda for a household. Now, I learned that marriage was something both parties had to fight for – not opposing each other – together, partners, fighting forces unseen. The marriage class taught us about ancient covenants, how the people who entered them were ready to die protecting them. I was fighting for our marriage and could sure feel the opposition, but we were not beside each other in the trenches.

I have learned that God doesn't have to use a lot of words. Just a few say so much. The words he gave me during this confusing time were simple, "watch his actions." So, I did, and what I saw was a revelation. I felt less confused when words weren't considered. I watched and learned and felt a deeper sadness dawning. My husband did not love me, despite his words to the contrary. His actions spoke volumes.

We had planned a trip to California for his niece's high school graduation and then as a result of our separation, downgraded it to two separate trips, me to Maine with our oldest and he to California with our youngest. He wasn't willing to reconsider our plans now, even though our separation was over, and we were supposedly back on better footing. It was a warning flag to me, and I asked him the night before we left if he was going to see anyone else in California, namely a woman he had an affair with before I met him.

"Why would I want to do that," he said, brushing off my question as if I was crazy. In fact, over the years, he had a way of making me feel crazy for many of my own thoughts or hunches. His penchant for rewriting history, and mine for external locus of control, made us a perfect, dysfunctional couple.

Anyway, we went our separate ways to vacation. Maine was beautiful, and it was good to have a little time with just my oldest daughter, now seven-and-a-half. A time of wonder and joy, our feet in the ocean until it was too cold to stand.

He hadn't called, and I knew he wasn't anxious to pay the roaming charges required in that day, but I really wanted to talk to him on the long drive home. He cut me off after only a few minutes, and again I felt the warning flag. I was longing to see him, and the feeling wasn't mutual.

Back home again and unpacking, I found a movie in my youngest's suitcase. It was really a stupid, little thing, but for some reason, I felt my hackles rise. It was a DVD of *Cinderella*, and when I asked her about it, she said it was from a friend of Daddy's in California. I asked her enough to know who the *friend* was, and felt my whole world crashing in. *Cinderella*, the ultimate fairy tale that makes little girls long for romance and marriage, was a gift from his former lover. The one I'd asked about the night before he left. As soon as the plane touched down, they'd driven to her home. He'd told me a boldface lie and had only said he would lie again whenever the truth was difficult. This was a man who wanted an easier way. The scorpion who stung the turtle after crossing the river on its back – that was a story he loved to tell. I hated that story, but he was trying to tell me something and I wasn't listening.

I packed a suitcase for him and delivered it to the trunk of his car at work. I called and asked him not to come home. I needed some time to think. He tried to tell me nothing had happened, and used the line of logic that our daughter had been with him, how could he have had an affair given that?

I didn't buy it, and I couldn't forgive him for taking our little five-year-old into his lie, then having the nerve to use her as his escape clause. I only asked for some time to think, but he came back home, rolling over my boundary, wondering if we could stay married, but sleep in different bedrooms. For the umpteenth time in our relationship, I felt completely unknown. I want to be in a union with integrity, and shared lives, and mutual love. Trouble is, I had never asked for it. I had never really revealed who I was to him, and I certainly hadn't attracted him with my integrity. So, although his request was another red flag, the truth of things became a still clearer, and I began to see why it was such a mistake to spin around in the distance dance, keeping my heart hidden. That was progress, although I had so far to go.

The actual divorce took almost another year and a half. I thought the hard part was over once he filed, but how could I know I had just entered a war zone with the worst collateral damage yet to come? Even in this chapter's writing, I feel ragged and dirty; stained in a way that only fighting for your life by hurting others can make you feel. But my best advisors, my most Godly friends, all said the same, *you have to fight*. Me. The peacemaker, the conflict-avoider, the people pleaser, the journalist skilled at seeing an issue from every possible angle; the overweight, burned-out, broken mother of two.

I had to pick myself up and war.

My first marriage had lasted six years. It seemed loud and my divorce quiet. We had no children, and no assets to speak of. Now, I'd had a comparatively quiet marriage of almost 10 years where arguments had only arisen occasionally as the baggage gathered beneath the rug. I was naïve enough to assume that we would sit down, make agreements, and move on. Wrong.

He hired an attorney and started making other strategic moves, like asking me to sign a statement saying I had no ownership in the company I helped him start. That was the beginning of my hunch that money and property were more valuable than I.

I thought it made sense for the girls to stay with me during the week to keep their school lives stable, but we couldn't agree. At one point, he calmly suggested I might go home to my parents 700 miles away without the girls! I was not just shocked; red flags went off over my entire body. *What were his true thoughts and motives, and who did he think I was?*

We had recently purchased a little lake house to renovate, hoping to flip it for profit in six months. He agreed to pay the mortgage and I the costs of rehab out of profits. After the bathrooms were installed, I decided to move there, and we divided our household goods and separated again. We agreed the lake house would become mine in the divorce, and our home, his.

At one point, we went to see a mediator and it didn't go well. We sat out in the car afterwards and I told him all I wanted was enough to buy a small house and the ability to have the girls during the week, offering him weekends and holidays. He didn't agree, and so we proceeded to family court, then financial settlement, then divorce finally toward the end of 2004.

One of the costliest decisions of my life – emotionally and financially – was hiring an attorney, supposedly the best attorney in our community for custody cases, who never gave me any advice of value for the kids, but went after the financial settlement like a bear. I could have had alimony and a larger settlement, but finally said, "This is enough!" and walked away from the financial mediation, thoroughly disgusted with the process, myself and my attorney.

During the hateful time I walked in and out of so-called "family" court and fought the battles that would ensue even after divorce, my husband seemed dedicated to my destruction. I've often wondered if what I encountered was an active, intentional hatred or an absolute vacuum of any feelings at all. Family court was across from one of the largest cemeteries in town. I made a covenant with my eyes to never look at court if I could look at the cemetery instead. The death on one side of the road was far more terrible than the graves on the other.

He carried our health insurance and had me removed from the policy. I discovered it months later, and was reinstated, without any consequences for him, even though what he had done was illegal. He told me that my parents didn't love me; told me that he had a black book filled with all my misdeeds; tried to get the courts to open medical records several times, telling me I would be declared an unfit mother. I was under assault and in my better moments recognized my battle wasn't against flesh and blood (Ephesians 6:12). It felt like spiritual darkness, and prayer seemed to be the only way to keep from stepping on landmines.

THE WAY OUT AND THE WAY IN

I sat down once with both my pastor and dear mentor and friend, Mary Bonham, laying out on a conference table a set of eight or so index cards, each with a complexity threatening the girls and I, each which seemed to have no solution. They just shook their heads, and my pastor said something I will always remember. He took the cards in his hands and looked me in the eye, tears in his own. "I can't tell you what to do, but I believe God has a solution for every single thing you face, and I will pray."

It was not a solution or a pat answer; it was *the only answer*: 'Not by might nor by power, but by my Spirit,' says the LORD (Zech. 4:6). God knew the way I had taken into this situation, and in his great mercy for a redeemed sinner like me, God knew the way out.

My back was against the wall, and I had a choice before me: faith or bitter defeat. I chose faith and have never been sorry.

After "family" court – the black day I was told by a "referee," I better give my husband full joint custody and argue no more, I felt shamed. I had no voice it seemed. What I was asking for was logical and good for our young daughters. I knew it with every fiber of my being, but because he wanted joint custody, he seemed to be the darling of the court. I had to excuse myself from the courtroom to weep after being threatened into silence. Mary was there to pick me up and hold me together, offering healing words as she had so often, but I was smashed to pieces. How could this be God's will?

My husband called me that day after court to ask if I was okay. It struck me as completely outrageous. *No, I'm not okay, and I'll never be okay, and you have no right to ever ask me such a question again*, I yelled, crying, and hung up. I was getting angrier by the day.

In God's economy, I was walking around and around in a desert learning to trust:

> *Remember how the Lord your God led you through the wilderness for these forty years, humbling you and testing you to prove your character, and to find out whether or not you would obey his commands. Yes, he humbled you by letting you go hungry and then feeding you with manna, a food previously unknown to you and your ancestors. He did it to*

teach you that people do not live by bread alone; rather, we live by every word that comes from the mouth of the Lord. Deuteronomy 8:2-3 NLT

I'm not suggesting that God caused all these things to happen, but I am saying that he used these circumstances I found myself in to humble, test, and find out if I was listening. He caused me to be hungry for something more than I had been satisfied with, then let me learn how good and satisfying his words are.

The ink wasn't dry on our parenting time agreement, a complicated document to begin with, when our youngest told me that they were moving north 65 miles to live with Dad's girlfriend. She had a dog too, and wasn't it grand? I had known he was seeing someone, because one day he asked to revisit the list I had made of differences between us that needed to be dealt with if our marriage was going to work. Back then, he hadn't taken it seriously; now, he pulled it out and asked me to talk about it again, saying maybe more understanding would help him with his next relationship, even if it couldn't help us. I'm pretty certain my mouth actually dropped open in disbelief. He wanted me to help him with his next girlfriend but wasn't willing to work on our marriage? Needless to say, I wasn't willing to become his relationship advisor.

Anyway, the announcement about the move helped me make sense of why he had fought so hard for custody, and I was so grateful that, by God's grace, staying in our local public-school system was part of our court-ordered agreement. If it hadn't been ordered, I'm pretty sure my girls would have lost not only their home, but also their community, friendships and schools.

Because he had hidden his planned move and was taking our girls to live with his girlfriend, I filed a motion asking to change the custody agreement, but by the time the court heard it six months later, was told that the girls were now 'accustomed' to the agreement and it wouldn't be good to make changes. More money and time down the drain. I felt naïve and powerless. I was fighting for everything I was worth, literally and metaphorically, but I continued to lose battles.

And so, the girls drove 130 miles each day to school and back during their father's hard-fought equal parenting time. There was never enough patience to wait for them to join after-school activities or sports, however much I wanted it, at least not until they were in their teens. Then, they were old enough to voice it if they wanted to stay with me overnight, and thank God for the volleyball, NHS, school musicals and swimming that followed. But at the time of the divorce, they were only seven-and-a-half and 10.

As the litter of divorce continued its ugly swirl, my oldest had to give her horse away, another painful episode. Now, he reasoned with a child – one spending more than two hours a day on the road to school and back during his weeks, "You never want to go see her," suggesting they give the horse to someone who would care better for it. The horse was boarded miles from his girlfriend's home, and my suspicion was always that he was the one who didn't want to go see the horse or pay for boarding and food once the challenge of keeping his promise got real.

In a final insult to his own integrity, my attorney submitted the signed divorce decree to the courts missing a few critical pages: There was nothing about the lake house, my largest asset. I found out that day because I went to the courthouse to look at the document he had filed – although now I can't remember why. Perhaps it was another answer to prayer for light on the path. I must have asked for light on the path a million times. Fortunately, the judge hadn't signed it yet, or I would have had to go back to court again. Caught between utter disbelief and flaming anger, I learned that you can't just "fire" an attorney, the court has to agree to a change. After the corrected settlement was filed and the divorce decree final, I exited the toxic relationship with my attorney. There was another fire that had to be put out, but I would find someone new to fight that battle. I was getting some wisdom, but it was definitely the hard way.

Prior to the divorce becoming final, my husband had let the mortgage on the lake house go unpaid despite a court order to the contrary. I came home one day to find a sheriff's sale notice on my door. Our little home was in foreclosure and would be sold within weeks. I called him in disbelief, and he said he didn't care if the kids and I were out on the street. The truth is, I think he did care. He thought that if I couldn't provide for them, the courts would award him custody. Anyway, the sheriff sale happened, and my house, the largest piece of my divorce settlement was sold, jerked like a rug from under my feet. Had God not so powerfully taught me to trust him, I can only imagine how I would have fallen into the black hole again.

When the divorce was finally, *correctly* filed, I went to a new attorney promising payment out of funds I hadn't received yet, and she graciously took me on. Undoing what had been done in the foreclosure was expensive, but it secured a home and a stable financial future for the girls and me.

As my funds from the settlement did come in, I paid full tithe on every single penny I received, just as I had and would continue to pay tithe on any other financial gains I experienced. There was more than a little appropriate defiance in my heart as I wrote those checks: God was my help, not this bitterly fought money!

Finally, the lake house renovations were complete, and it sold. I was able to buy a home from the profit in the same neighborhood where each of my girls had a friend. Their friends came over, and we had a little party and home dedication.

The fears written on each of the index cards were resolved, one-by-one, by a God who knew the way. Slowly I was learning I could lean on him, wait for him to act and shed light on my next steps. I could trust him to fight my battles. The words I had heard early on in recovery from the mouth of Sandy Burdick, the founder of *Open Hearts Ministry*, became my own. They were written deep on my heart and gave courage when everything seemed to be falling apart:

> *I would have despaired unless I had believed that I would see the goodness of the Lord in the land of the living. Wait for the Lord; Be strong and let your heart take courage; Yes, wait for the Lord.* (Psalm 27:13-14 NASB)

That was more than 15 years ago, and there have been plenty of things I haven't understood since, believe me! But God has given me an appreciation for mystery. An ability to trust what I cannot comprehend, and patiently wait for his action. I have seen his power in the midst of tragedy and cruelty. I have seen him bring good out of what others meant for evil.

Because of the road I've walked, I trust he knows every scenario, every possibility, every contingency. He is literally the only one who has been to hell and come back, carrying the keys (Revelation 1:18), and thus can help us find *the way through hell and the way back home.*

Chapter 9: Does God Really Have a Plan?
(Because This Seems Like Chaos!)
QUESTIONS FOR REFLECTION

Question: When have you longed for "milk and honey" but found a war instead? How did you respond and if you found the strength, how did you fight it?

Question: Did you ever have a significant person in your life teach you how to do hard things? If so, who? What did they teach you and how might it help out with situations you now face?

Question: Scripture says that hope that is seen is not hope at all (Romans 8:24), yet we want to see hope, success, dreams come true – and we often judge God when things don't evolve that way. How do you interpret faith being the assurance of what is not seen (Hebrews 11:1)?

Action: Write each of your biggest fears or challenges out on a separate notecard, then pray over them, even with a friend you trust. Put them in a place where you'll remember to find them, pray over them again, and note the answers when they come.

I close my eyes,
whisper Your name
Hold out my arms
You do the same
I rest my head
on Your beating heart
Rhythm so strong
Here in my dark

I close my eyes, and
ask for your hand
I ask for your will
'Cause I trust Your plan
No longer afraid,
'cause You're never far
I'm never alone
'Cause we're never apart, so

Now I lay me down to sleep
And pray the Lord my soul to keep
If I should die before I wake
I know the Lord my soul will take
When I close my eyes...
Yes, I close my eyes.

April 2006

Chapter 10
Is God Really Good? Can God be Trusted?

There are many more stories of these painful years.
They could fill this whole book, but that's not what this
book is about. This book is about how falls happen.
Sometimes because you get pushed, sometimes because
you accidentally trip, and sometimes because you're trying
to walk in the dark. It's about how redemption is hard, and
sometimes you hurt a long time and nothing good seems to
happen. Sometimes, like the children of Israel, you find
yourself wondering if God really cares or knows what to
do, so you ask, "Did you bring me out here just to let me
die? Are you *really* good? Can I trust you completely?"
    Sometimes you have to just walk around the same 200
miles of desert, dust choking your nostrils, when you'd

rather be floating above it all in a hot-air balloon, or rising beyond its heat and thirst in the miracle of free flight.

Still, this is *the mystery*. If I had set out to write a mystery novel, the juxtaposition of growth from death would have made great grist for the mill because, despite all the terrible things that happened, my faith grew. Sometimes the truth really is stranger than fiction.

TRUST IN THE DARK

God had a penchant for bringing wonderful men and women into our lives, and the girls and I got front row seats to watch faith in action. Every time I wanted to write men off, God showed me a trustworthy man. When the courts didn't enforce child support payments for six months, we found groceries on our front porch, and a small group from church "adopted" us for Christmas. We received so many gift cards, they filled an envelope to overflowing and lasted far longer than Christmas, but I was able to buy the girls wonderful presents just before the big day. One friend's husband came by to remove a bat I found hanging over me one morning during a quiet time – and we called "batman" for several rescue missions. Others helped with home maintenance issues and packing and moving when the lake house finally sold. One friend did work for me over the course of the next decade, sometimes for pay, sometimes just out of kindness.

One time my van died and neighbors from church just gave me theirs – simply saying they didn't need it anymore! One time when I didn't have any money for the fight ahead, a new friend gave me an incredibly large sum of money to retain an attorney. I resisted, but she told me God had asked her to do this. I learned that the circle of giving can't be complete without receivers. That truth was like an arrow to the marrow for me, the one who hated being needy. Being in need wasn't contrary to God's plan, sometimes it was part of his plan as he worked his will out in lives besides mine. I began to form a theology of need and abundance – God's economy, even if that's not what I called it.

I had witnessed the devastation to children when moms had to go to work fulltime after a divorce. I wanted to always be there for the girls after school, and by God's grace was able to cobble together freelance, temp work, or part time jobs that made that possible for the duration of their years before college, almost a decade. Until they were in middle school and early high school, I tried to never be gone in the evenings, making exceptions only for recovery groups, which I often helped co-lead, or worship team rehearsal, when they could be involved in children's ministry or youth group.

For a year or more, my recovery group of choice was *DivorceCare*, where I co-led with a dear friend who is still like a beloved sister to me. We processed our own losses over late-night cups of tea, sometimes laughing, sometimes crying. In group, we heard many good teachings that helped us avoid common traps and many tragic stories that reminded us we were not alone.

Rebound relationships were a trap I saw a lot of divorced women fall into. I had done that too, without unpacking the pain of my past and understanding of my own part in the wreckage, and I didn't need to do it again. It was just so easy to think it was all the other person's problems, and that this time I would simply pick more wisely. But I learned that history has a way of repeating itself – especially if you fell into the trap of making your history all bad. I learned that you have to find the good too if you are to emerge better able to discern good from bad.

I had a tough time finding good but with God's help and recovery ministries such as *DivorceCare* and *OHM,* began to pick my failures apart until I understood where my own faults and weaknesses were. I had to answer the question *what makes me so vulnerable to pain in my occupation and relationships?*

God began to address my naiveté in relationships – about assuming others were operating on the same playing field as I. *If I am nice, others will be nice to me.* Instead of staying safe, I attracted people who intuited my "niceness," (a word I've come to mistrust!) as a signal that I could be taken advantage of. I had to learn the difference between safe people and wounded people, and how often "hurt people hurt people." Often, it's a matter of testing relationships much like Joseph tested his brothers before revealing to them who he was (Genesis 42-45). First, we have to get over thinking others think just like us, and then we need a framework to help identify what safe people look like, interact like, connect like. Then, we can start building a circle of friends who are trustworthy, people who keep their word and speak honestly to us, even if it hurts. *Faithful are the wounds of a friend, but deceitful are the kisses of an enemy* (Proverbs 27:6 NASB), said Solomon. A lot of time in *OHM* small groups where accountability kept people honest and real, and one short book, *Safe People*, by Henry Cloud and John Townsend, put my feet on a better path.

Early on, I desired to date again – and someday, to have a marriage like I believed was possible – but I also knew the extent of my brokenness. Healing was more important, and I knew the girls needed both my healing *and* my undivided attention. I asked God only once if he would bring me a true son of his, then told him I would be quiet and not ask again. I got a little impatient at times, but for the most part, that subject was off the table between us. I honestly didn't believe I deserved another marriage; but I always believed in marriage. It was sacred, and meaningful, and if God allowed it, I would too.

A sense of excitement about God's enigmatic ways was growing. In those years, whenever something bad would happen, I would say to the girls, "Now, watch! Let's pray and see how God is going to work this out." And he would! It happened over and over, until my faith was strong. I had stories of deliverance of my own. I had stories to share. I had something to give away. I had something to "treasure up in my heart" like Mary of old, even if it had been born out of pain and need. I was getting a little nearer to the Promised Land. My mothers' prayer, even now, is that someday the girls will remember all the times God brought good out of what seemed bad or impossible. It may be awhile, I understand that, because their lives were deeply impacted by the divorce, and in ways I wasn't. Their prayers for parents that stayed together weren't answered. Maybe God seems capricious as they try to put together their pain with the God who answers prayers. Maybe God seems confusing as they look back at a Mom who was there for them, but often in tears, and often hurt by the latest offense dished up by divorce and immediate replacement. Their dad and I operated our homes very differently, and that was undoubtedly a source of uncertainty and pain as they grew up. My youngest called, crying sometimes, for me to come get her and I couldn't. It was hard on her, and equally hard on me. I felt ambivalent and powerless to stop the chaos. Ultimately, I felt the sting of their anger as I've tried to walk a tightrope between honesty and encouraging them to love their father and stepmother. I've failed to stay silent sometimes when I should have. I've failed to have the peace and contentment that could have made the journey easier for them. It was available to me through the goodness of God, but so many times I couldn't appropriate it and that makes me sad.

Still, even if they can't see it, I can see God was with us. Somehow, through the darkness and the minefields I navigated, he was leading me step by step. My cry, over and over, "give me light," was answered continuously, in the most miraculous ways.

SHEDDING THE PERSONA

During these years, things were happening at the micro level in my heart. Obviously, I was crying again, and crying was catharsis. It softened my heart toward my own story, helping the girl I once had been to re-emerge, even if there was a lot of damage to her. The truth is, before you can heal, you have to own and examine the damage. That can't happen when you're hiding.

Coming out of hiding meant the beginnings of retrieving that little girl who had split – humorously also a 1960s term for "let's get out of here!" When I gave her up, it was as if I had given up my internal compass. Reclaiming her was like discovering all over again who God had made me to be. I wish I could say it happened all at once, but like rebuilding, it happened in stages, sometimes with the work of an archeologist, sometimes an architect, sometimes a wrecking ball. God has both rebuilt on ruins and started new things. Even today, the work continues as I come out from slavery to pleasing, hiding, pretending, and self-protection. Those were the survival strategies of my persona, and gratefully, they are being shed like old skin cells.

My love for music and dreams of songwriting were reborn. After the healing journey that began in 2003, I went to my first-ever songwriting conference. I walked through the doors of Belmont College in Nashville and wandered around after registration. A young girl, maybe 17, walked in with her parents and I greeted them. She looked nervous, guitar in hard, but greeted me too. "My name is Francesca Battistelli," she said, sticking out her free hand, "What's yours?" How could I ever forget that name? My brush with greatness continued. I saw pure faith, hard work, and flaming egos as the GMA event unfolded. I saw wannabes like me, trying to hold our own in the sea of greatness. But the best and loudest voice I brought home with me was Pastor Scotty Smith's. At some point in those years, God began speaking to me more through preaching than even music, and I was amazed that at a songwriting workshop, it was the preacher who touched my life in such a profound way.

I had just written a song called *To This Well*, and on Saturday morning, Scotty preached on the very same woman at the well. He was telling my story it seemed, a woman scorned, in shame, going from marriage to marriage looking for love and life, finding loss and brokenness. But oh, the glorious redemption. A woman Jesus doesn't scorn, a woman he woos instead, speaking truth into her life in a way that transforms her, catalyzing her testimony as she becomes the first missionary of the gospel. That gave me hope. Filled with that hope, the next morning I drove to the church Scotty pastored, Christ Community Church in Franklin. Again, he breathed the hope of gospel into me, and afterwards, I sought him out, and he prayed over me and my story. It was my birthday, and the beginning of a trend. Every birthday, God would give me a special hug, known only to him and me. Scotty's prayer and conversation were my hug that day.

During the separation, I had prayed for a co-writer and written a bunch of lyrics with that in mind. No co-writer ever appeared, so I sat down at my digital piano and began to play. The painful reality that I was without my daughters half the time –and my nearest family 700 miles away – was very tangible. I avoided full-time work and social engagements so I could be there for the girls, but they were 65 miles away *half the time*. Those days a wall of grief would hit me, overwhelm me, and I would cry for hours at a time. I would avoid their rooms, sometimes even closing the doors in an attempt to shut out my grief and loss. That end of the hall represented my failure, restarting that old recording again, *whatever I touch will be hurt, something is wrong with me.*

The worst time would be a holiday when they were with their Dad for a week or more. Even if they were with him on vacation, in Florida or Washington D.C. for example, I couldn't shake the feeling that I should be home, waiting for them, there if they needed me. So, I sat down in my loneliness and tears, and wrote music. Tunes flowed toward lyrics, and I recorded a CD project called *Secret Closet* in 2007, chronicling my painful journey back toward God from childhood abuse, divorce, and dysfunction. Not filled with chart toppers, as you can imagine!

When the girls were gone, I learned to go to movies alone (arrive late, slip into the back, then leave as soon as the credits roll), to restaurants alone (often with a book or my computer), and to church alone (where people loved me anyway). So, one spring break I thought, *why not try a vacation alone*? I went to Florida, to an area I had taken the girls several years before. I holed up in a hotel and wrote for most of a week. For breaks, I walked the beach, sat and watched the ocean, and found a restaurant with incredible little tacos where I ate every night.

That week I began work on a novel, and the days flew. I missed the girls and home but felt victorious because I hadn't sat home all week and cried. It was the beginning of seeking life again. I often said that I made up for all the decades I hadn't cried by crying for about five years. Then, one day, I felt the Lord nudge me. I heard something like, *I delivered you, but you don't ever feel the joy of that. You are so focused on what you lost that you've forgotten how I answered your prayers.* It was a good reminder, and even when joy continues to be a struggle, I remember God's words. They come to me when I feel sorry for myself, or like I am the victim in all the stories of my life. Then, I began see that my life mattered to God, and while I wasn't full of passion and purpose, I believed he had his reasons that I was still alive. I became riveted by the desire to "take hold of that for which Christ Jesus took hold of me (Philippians 3:12 NIV)."

After those years in mourning, I noticed that I began to struggle with co-leading in the recovery ministry. I had attended and/or co-led more than 25 of these groups over the years, hearing stories of hundreds of people who had experienced abuse and/or trauma in their childhood, frequently mixed up with spiritual abuse of some kind. It was a lot to process while going through personal trauma *and* unpacking my own childhood abuse. I think it helped me keep my own journey in perspective, and it definitely gave me a place to give back what I'd been given. But, in the end, my heart began to need something fresh and new, and ultimately this was the journey that led to seminary and the work I am involved in today.

I had learned something about the goodness of God. About how his purposes were good, even if it was dark around me. I learned to let him hold my hand and lead the way out of the valley of the shadow of death. I got a little closer to the Promised Land.

Chapter 10: Is God Really Good? Can God be Trusted?
QUESTIONS FOR REFLECTION

Question: What are you the most hungry for – food notwithstanding? Could your hunger be drawing you to God? Explain.

Question: Have you been a giver or a receiver most often? Are both necessary in God's economy?

Question: Do you feel particularly vulnerable to pain in your occupation and/or relationships? Can you pick apart any "whys"?

Question: What part of you is "persona" and what part of you is able to be honest with your emotions? Draw a pie chart and label it if that helps you visualize the parts.

Question: What do you do with your loneliness? What could you do with it that would drive you more deeply into God's purposes, even if you're in the darkest, loneliest spot of your life?

Question: Rate your trust for God on a scale of 1 to 10 (1 being non-existent). Why?

Something to ponder: During my healing journey I learned that all longings, at their core, are good. Core longings are basic human needs for love, safety, acceptance, to be understood, significance, and purpose, and when not met, drive all kinds of crazy behaviors. If I could trace the behaviors that I disliked in myself (or others) back to a core longing, I could understand myself better and acknowledge what I was most in need of. Whatever makes you over-the-top angry, desperately sad, or totally numb will give you a clue into what core longing is driving your behavior. (An example: I hate being embarrassed. I turn red, get ashamed and/or angry, and hide my true self when it happens. I might dislike all those responses, but when I realized that my core longings were to be understood and safe, I could handle myself differently, asking God and others for what I really needed.)

Action: Read the short book "Safe People" by Henry Cloud and John Townsend. How are your skills at being a safe person for others and attracting safe friends for yourself?

I've seen some strong hearts broken by this crazy world
When the place of sanctuary became the eye of storm
But I've also seen the mystery of Your love reaching down
Into chaos, and darkness, and pain You make your own...so

It isn't done
Until You say it's done;
Until Your work is finished, and
My last, hard race is run.
I need those eagle's wings
And fiercer Spirit winds
And strength to rise again
Until You say it's done.

September 2014

Chapter 11
How Will God Ever Complete the Work Started in Me?

My involvement on the worship team grew, even as my faith did. I absolutely loved it, and in those hours of song and service, I had a peace I rarely found anywhere else. If I wasn't on the team, I sat through the service, typically crying. It seemed like I couldn't help it. When I entered the worship center, I just started crying. I know it aggravated the girls – especially my youngest, who would try to get me to wipe my tears and buck up. My oldest seemed to feel with me more, and as she matured, would often cry too as she worshipped. What a tender heart she had, especially for God's creation and creatures. She was very spiritually attuned from an early age, and told me at about age three, "Mom, did you know there are three Gods? They all live up there and work together." How I loved that little girl and her tender heart. She made me remember what was good and pure about the world. She made me long to be a better person.

Both had asked Jesus to come live in their hearts around age five, and my oldest baptized as soon as she made that decision. My youngest, though, was feisty and skeptical, with God and me. She loved practical jokes and told lies, it seemed, just because she could. "Mom, it's opposites day," she would announce, then tell a whopper just for fun. She told me at about age five, "Mom, I don't get God, he's just too darn clear!" Then, in middle school she announced on the way home one day, "Mom, I just love sarcasm, it's my new favorite!" She was finally baptized around age 10 but had put it off so many times at that point, I wasn't certain it would happen until the moment the water rolled down her face! I couldn't help but love that little rascal. She helped me remember what was funny and satirical about the world. How she has made me laugh!

Throughout the years, my passion for worship leading continued to grow, and two pastors planting churches asked if I would come and lead their congregations. I said no, although it was one of the hardest things I'd ever done. I didn't feel ready and was deeply skeptical of doing anything again that I wasn't prepared for. I led for women's groups, and for the recovery ministry of which I was part. And, after serving on teams for years, was finally trusted to lead worship on Sundays when the worship director was gone.

God had done quite a work in me before that happened. In 2002 when I started my healing journey, I hadn't really played the piano for about 15 years, and even then, I wasn't very good. I had a few lessons as a child and taught myself to chord at about age 20, knowing that classical music would never be my passion. Now, about four years after I started playing again, I sat at the beautiful grand piano in our worship center and felt God asking me to trust him with my hands. I decided to do that, to just let go of what I knew and what I didn't and lean into what God knew about music – which was everything. I began experiencing more freedom, was able to lead and write better. No, I wasn't suddenly a professional musician, but God was equipping the called rather than calling the equipped. I got a little closer to the Promised Land.

I still enjoy leading worship as often as I get the chance. There is a freedom that tastes like peace and rest; a connection between God and his people that feels like a call.

NOT DONE

At a Global Leadership Summit, perhaps 2007, I had one of those moments that comes back to you over the years; a powerful word that feels like a call. Author and Pastor John Ortberg was speaking and said passionately, almost as an aside, "If you are a woman God has called to lead, for heaven's sake! Lead!" I burst out into tears, those words reverberated so deeply in my spirit, calling forth hope that was painful amidst shattered dreams. There were other words like that too, reminders that God wasn't finished with me. Powerful treasures in my pocket. God's special words to my heart. You know you've heard, because they penetrate more deeply than any arrow if you choose to let them in. But this is also true: Hope hurts. Coming alive to who you are, to the dreams God has planted in your heart since the day you were born hurts. That's because that hope has the power to make you feel vulnerable to loss again.

Growing up for me has meant embracing the ambivalence that so often collides in my chest. I can hope and be afraid at the same time. I can take risks and know I may fail at the same time. I can feel joy and sorrow at the same time and live through it – holding on to what I know is true. Paul once said that there is a sorrow that leads to death and a sorrow that leads to life (2 Corinthians 7:10), and I've found that I can live with the latter which he calls "repentance without regret." What a beautiful concept! I began to learn that Christian hope flows out of the work God is doing and has done to rebuild me, all that walking around in sand, that wrecking ball, that excavation – he is the architect of my future:

> *We can rejoice, too, when we run into problems and trials, for we know that they help us develop endurance. And endurance develops strength of character, and character strengthens our confident hope of salvation. And this hope will not lead to disappointment.* Romans 5:3-5 NLT

That's a great definition of the training program of God. Endurance and persistence lead to strength of character, and that's exactly what God is searching for. We become people of a hope that won't disappoint – why? Because we are longing for what God longs for too. The writer of Hebrews teaches that hope is tied to faith (Hebrews 11:1), we may not see what we long for now, or ever, but if we are longing for what God created us to be, we will see it someday. With Paul, I can say, "I know the one in whom I trust, and I am sure that he is able to guard what I have entrusted to him until the day of his return (2 Timothy 1;12 NLT)."

In worship, and in the challenge of leading others into God's presence, I began to sense my calling. I saw the church as distracted in worship, desiring an experience more than a real relationship with a fiery and jealous God. I began to form a theology of worship, even though I didn't know that's what it was. I saw that people could only worship as large as the God they believed in, and it seemed through my story that God was calling me to paint a bigger picture of that amazing bigness and exhort people to move closer.

Many Christians in America live in a narrow box all their lives, self-sufficient, never really understanding their need or desperation for God. Some hide behind masks of perfection, afraid to let their wounds be known. They don't experience what Scripture teaches, that it's only through him that everything around us is holding together (Colossians 1:17). They go through the motions of worship and prayer, listening to sermons week after week, only to go home and forget what they heard, living largely self-reliant lives. Like a person who looks into a mirror, then immediately forgets what he/she looks like (Jm. 1:23-24). After all my own pain, I had no such illusions; I believed in an immense God and I was ultra-clear that *it was not me*.

I was asked for a third time to lead, this time at a church torn by a split. It sounded just like divorce to me, and I saw a place where God could use the gifts and story he'd given me, an opportunity to help the hurting congregation who'd been left behind. It was during this six month "loan" from my own congregation that I first started thinking about seminary. I deeply desired more education and felt like I had always been caught between my confident exterior and fearful interior in my jobs. This was one of the ways I was always vulnerable. My ethos was girl spinning, confident, energetic; my pathos was girl falling, lacking preparation, not knowing what to do when things got tough.

I wanted training but couldn't find a graduate program that interested me. The day I went up to the seminary's website and read course curriculum it was like a light had turned on. *This was it!* I thought, closely followed by *whatever would a seminary do with me, a twice-divorced woman?* Dreams are as powerful as childhood vows, though. I began to investigate, talking with a few pastor friends and then the director of admissions at Western Theological Seminary, Rev. Dr. Mark Poppen, who became a dear friend and voice of truth in my life over the next six years. Mark told me he needed a ride on his motorcycle one day, so he covered the 50-plus miles and many potholes between us in order to answer my questions about the seminary journey. Over the years he spoke into my life at critical junctures, helping me understand more about God's call and the importance of critical thinking as I tried to keep my faith afloat in the cerebral world of academia. There were potholes to be navigated there too, and his voice of experience blessed me.

In 2009, I began the long journey toward a Master of Divinity with a single class in the newly formed distance learning curriculum. God had opened every door, just like a gentleman; my *Ish* (the name of God that means husband). At every turn in the admission process and journey of coming under student care of my church's governing body, I told my story. At every turn, I expected to be rejected, but somehow, it never happened. The leader, an older pastor who could have easily dismissed me, said "I think people need to hear your story." A pastor-mentor introduced me at a dinner to welcome new students, calling me, "the real deal."

Only my own pastor issued a word of caution, "If you're going to become a pastor, you've got to toughen up," he said. He had watched my journey for almost a decade now, so if anyone would know, I guess it would be him. Strangely, he was shortly an instrument of toughening and I began to realize that a lot of people will champion you when you're down, but when you try to move forward again, it sometimes requires a new group of champions. It's hard for people who've witnessed you completely broken to believe God can restore you for something big, like seminary or pastoral ministry. Heck, it was hard for *me* to believe. Why would I fault others?

I had led part-time at the church that suffered the split for six months when it was announced that the old congregation would fold, and a church plant would be launched there by my home congregation. Immediately, I felt a surge of excitement that I would likely be asked to be part of the plant. I fell asleep that night excited about the future. Seminary, and a potential job as worship leader for a new church plant. That night I had a strange dream, and when I woke up, the knowledge was as clear as a bell that I needed to prepare my heart – I was not going to be invited. I even knew who would be asked. I had been warned by God in a dream and would need to go a different way. Wow, it hurt, and I think if God hadn't called me first, and then warned me so kindly, the bitterness of those broken dreams could have easily taken root. The lies were right there. *You're not valuable, you're not worth it, you won't ever get it right.* But the voice of truth told me a different story.

I went back to my home congregation, eventually serving on the team and even leading again. One particular Sunday, I was to lead both services with full orchestra. It was a lot and I was obviously in over my head. Still, I was determined to say 'yes' to whatever God had for me, so when my worship director asked, that's what I answered.

That morning, as I led, there were a group of men sitting across the front row to my right. Men of power – my pastor; the pastor of the new church plant; an elder and an associate pastor, both of whom had both made disparaging remarks that had come back to my ears. I was suddenly scared. So much was riding on my ability to please and impress them it seemed.

As soon as that thought crossed my mind, I heard a voice, "Are you here for me, or them?" Blessedly, I knew the answer, and deeply, for one of the first times in my life, the yoke of trying to please people was broken. God was changing and shaping me for the challenges that lay ahead. I can't say that I've never suffered from people pleasing again, but its grip on my life was broken, and I got a little nearer the Promised Land that morning.

A few months later, sitting in the pastor's study in a meeting with the worship leader and pastor, I got blown away, both metaphorically and literally. We met each time after I led, doing a SWAT analysis of the service. I often left demoralized, feeling like I was never enough, like I was being compared to the worship director instead of just celebrated for what I brought. A few things were said that day it would be hard to forget, primarily that my vocal ability just wasn't good enough and I was too old to lead. Sitting there between those two, both friends and mentors, after almost a decade of serving on teams and worshipping together – writing, singing, leading, growing, praying, encouraging, serving however I was asked – hearing those words was just stunning. I hadn't been running a competition, after all, just filling in for the worship director when he needed a break or a vacation. I wasn't on staff and wasn't expecting accolades. I just wanted to serve however I could. Yet I was being told that I was finished, and I couldn't discern if they would ever want me to serve again…anywhere…in our church. Nothing was mentioned.

Old lies rose up, threatening to choke me; but the truth rose up too. I had some news of my own. Yet another church had invited me to be their worship leader, so apparently, I was not too old or too shabby vocally for God.

Sometimes God moves us on. Sometimes it feels more like a shove. Still, I love those two. Despite this awful conversation, God used them for so much growth and good in my life. I would be a fool to discard the good with the bad.

That's the day I learned that even when the world (or the church) tells you you're through, you're not done until God says so. And it's a lesson I've needed to hear many times since. But every time I pick myself up and walk on, trusting God to finish the work started, I get a little closer to the Promised Land.

Chapter 11: How Will God Ever Complete the
Work Started in Me?
QUESTIONS FOR REFLECTION

Question: Is there any area of your life where you could let
go of fear and/or control and allow God more room?

Question: I said that "coming alive to who you are, to the
dreams God has planted in your heart since the day you
were born hurts. That's because hope has the power to
make you feel vulnerable to loss again." Where would
hoping for something make you feel most vulnerable?
Could you see hope as an act of Godly defiance?

Question: If it's true that God's training program is
"endurance and persistence lead to strength of character,
and that's exactly what God is searching for" where are you
in the training?

Action: In an act of defiant hope, revisit at least one
geographic location where you were told you weren't
enough. When you're there, in that place, ask the Lord of
Heaven and Earth what he would say to you, and listen –
and hold on. You're not done until God says you're done.

The winds will come, the storms will brew
The cold will cut me thru and thru
But I have found a place to stand
And I am standing firm on You.

I set my feet upon the Rock
I rest my head, I bow my heart
And there I breathe a victory song
I'm trusting strong and leaning hard into my God

Oh, I have tried building on sand
On distant shores, in distant lands
But grace has turned sins' tattered plans
And bid me welcome home again, so

My changing heart may shift again
But if I fail, this thing remains:
A perfect ransom paid by One
Who redeems saints and vagabonds

I set my feet upon the Rock
I rest my head, I bow my heart
And there I breathe a victory song
I'm trusting strong and leaning hard into my God
Oh I'm trusting strong and leaning hard into you, God.

August 2017

Chapter 12
How are Naïveté and Trust Different?

I'm sorry to bear the news that even the years that followed – four years as a worship director and a 50-hour master's degree from Western Theological Seminary in 2015 – have not inoculated me against vocational pain. Ministry is hard and I think that's what my pastor was trying to warn me of the day I looked for his blessing as I began seminary. His warning wasn't about the need for toughness to face a broken world as much as readiness to face a broken church.

In the world, we expect to get hurt, but in the church, it comes as a double whammy, shocking our faith with betrayal. David the songwriter put it like this: *It is not an enemy who taunts me— I could bear that. It is not my foes who so arrogantly insult me—I could have hidden from them. Instead, it is you—my equal, my companion and close friend* (Psalm 55:12-13).

Of course, I'm pretty certain that most of the people who've hurt me in ministry never thought of me as their equal, still, they felt like close friends who took shots. I needed to lose even more of the naiveté that characterized my thinking. After all, it was Jesus who said we must be wise as serpents *and* harmless as doves (Matthew 10:16), a both/and command, however bad being like a serpent might sound! Jesus also said he didn't need anyone to validate the truth about him or offer words of praise to bolster his self-esteem: *But Jesus didn't trust them, because he knew all about people. No one needed to tell him about human nature, for he knew what was in each person's heart.* (John 2:24-25 NLT) Jesus also made this astonishing comment that hasn't escaped my notice: *And it is true that the children of this world are more shrewd in dealing with the world around them than are the children of the light* (Luke 16:8 NLT).

I aspire to be more like Jesus in this, shrewd and harmless – but it's not one-and-done as much as it is a process. Maybe you didn't think sanctification included stealth operations, learning the politics of God rather than man, but I'm telling you it does. People's opinions will be as varied as the number of people around you, and sometimes you'll be the hero and sometimes the villainous crowd will want you crucified. Jesus knew that, and he's been trying to teach me too. He wasn't talking about the riffraff heathens; he was talking about crowds of *followers* who were gathering around him! The groupies. The social media followers. The people who could hide in the shadows, clicking smiley- and frowney-faces without ever entering the real battlefield.

The fresh realization that Satan was at work, even in the church, was startling; the reminder sobering that the target on my back was even clearer to the enemy as I drew closer to Jesus. Again and again, I've taken a hit, but gotten up to walk on, sheerly because I believed that if Satan was so determined to stop me, God must still have something he needed me to do.

I used to think it was naïve to trust anyone. New growth and wisdom have shaken the simple naiveté out of me, replaced with a hard-fought certainty that there is one who can be trusted, absolutely, even when the other voices fail, as they will, being only human. This does not mean it's the God-and-me show, it means that I am being trained in discernment and in keeping my ear tuned to God's Spirit (John 3:8). That voice will never lie, speak half-truths, or speak about what is only partially known. And that voice has taught me the importance of boundaries, testing relationships, and learning who is safe and can be trusted. Growth has come as I've learned to enter healthy conflict, letting in what's good and saying "no" more often.

Most of my vocation since I became an on-staff worship director in 2010 has been in ministry, although I've supplemented with a few part-time jobs outside of the church. I've been a worship director, a freelance writer for a denominational magazine, a devotional writer, a temporary staff member who helped implement a spiritual formation process, a small group leader, and am currently a ministry associate for a small church where I do communications work, a daily devotional, and anything else that needs to be done.

During that 10 years, I have been ignored because I was a woman (no, literally ignored, as in not even responded to when I asked a question), offered church discipline because I got angry about unfair treatment (wasn't allowed to explain my anger or work through the offense), told by an employer/pastor while in seminary that he had never offered to mentor me in ministry (as he refused to let me make a hospital visit with him to a member of our congregation who was dying), been disqualified as a candidate for worship leading jobs because I was a woman, and experienced numerous other wounds at the hands of church leadership.

The sad part is that every single woman I am close with after our years in seminary has stories of roadblocks thrown at them in ministry. And it's not just the women. The burnout rate of new pastors is legendary in the U.S.; I just happen to know a few women graduates and their stories. I'm not a pastor, having gotten a 50-hour Master of Arts rather than the Master of Divinity, but I am in ministry none-the-less, and I believe this is where God has called me: to the body of Christ and it's not a cakewalk.

The further along the journey of life I go, the fewer ideas of my own I act on; the more I am willing to just let God lead. It hasn't been to the heights of success I had dreamed of as a young person – a Nashville songwriter, or a prized author or worship leader sought out for conferences. But walking through doors God has opened, I have written my share of songs, sometimes ministering to the whole church, sometimes to people at a funeral, or to a happy couple saying, "I do." I've led worship for small and large crowds, retreats and conferences, women's groups and recovery groups. I've written several hundred devotions, a few poems, dramas and sermons, blogs, and copy for several ministry websites.

God has allowed me to experience great redemption from childhood abuse. The kind of redemption every victim longs for, but so few see. My abuser was sorry, acknowledging the harm to me and also telling my parents, and bringing forth fruit in keeping with repentance – the restitution that started my journey toward healing almost 20 years ago. My mother apologized for her part in the tangled mess, with tears, in her 80s. How I loved her for her honesty and grit in her senior years! I've had friends who have stuck with me through the worst of times, always ready to listen, cry with me, show me (and my daughters) the hands and feet of Jesus. And now, for almost a decade, God has allowed me to walk with an answer to my prayer so long ago, a true son of his – a faithful, God-loving man who knows everything about my story and still cheers me on in every way. I have let someone see who I really am and lived to tell!

It was clear to me from the start of the healing journey that in my woundedness and response to it, I had become blind. The real me went into hiding, the false self emerged, spinning an image of well-being and happiness. To project that image was to be busy with myself, never looking deeply at others or their motives; foolishly trusting they would care for me if I cared for them. Trying to keep myself and my secrets safe, I was every kind of naïve, and ultimately every kind of burned out and this precipitated so many of the falls in my life.

Learning to slow down, know God, and build trust again with safe others has been the work of my recovery. Now, I am equipped in two critical ways: First, I have an internal locus of control. I find my identity not in what others say about me, but what God says. Second, this shift has finally allowed me to walk in the freedom that Christ promises. I don't have to work so hard to understand what is going on around me so I can look perfect. I don't have to weary myself with glad-handing, spinning a picture of success in order to win approval. I can trust God for what is needed to finish the good work he started. I finally belong, just as I am, to him. That is true freedom – from my past, from my mistakes, from my Type A drive to succeed, from the pain of all the arrows meant to steal, kill and destroy, from fear of the future. I have rest!

God is the One, the only one, with power to determine the worth of a life. My times are in his fine hands (Psalm 31:15), and I am leaning hard on the truths that he has taught me so faithfully. I have found my peace with God, and it cannot be shaken.

Question: Write in your own words what it means to be both wise as a serpent *and* harmless as a dove (Matthew 10:16):

Question: Write one naïve belief you've held and write one sentence about something/someone you know you can trust. How have these beliefs shaped your life?

Question: Explain the difference between being naïve and trusting another. How are the two different? How might they be confused?

Action: Memorize one Scripture that contains a truth God speaks over you as his child. If you don't have a Bible, find a verse in this book – there are many. Write it here, and write not only the exact words, but also what they mean to you personally. Then commit it to memory so when a lie comes at you, you can speak the truth of God to it.

You wait, I wait
We bend so we don't break
And then we mend,
And try again for loves' sake
But it takes so long
To make us strong
In all the broken places
To learn mistakes belong
In songs, like lonely open spaces
So we wait in what remains
'Til melody erases pain

You hope, I hope
Through days alone
We'll find a way
Through this haze of heart and stone
But it takes so long
To make us strong
In all the broken places
To learn mistakes belong
In songs, like lonely open spaces
So we wait in what remains
'Til melody erases pain

On days I bear the weight of everything I feel
Oh I reach for you and swear
I'm getting lighter as I heal
Still it takes so long
To make us strong
In all the broken places
To learn mistakes belong
In songs, like lonely open spaces
So we wait in what remains
'Til melody erases pain
Oh we wait in what remains
Letting melody erase the pain

January 2011

Chapter 13
What Does Redemption Look Like?

I confess to being impatient. I think I've been that way all my life. Alabama made famous this lyric that reminds me of myself: "I'm in a hurry to get things done, oh I rush and rush until life's no fun. All I really gotta do is live and die, but I'm in a hurry and don't know why."

The rush for redemption was no different. As I began to unpack the damage, I was always pushing for redemption. *God, just get me past all this earth-bound walking; I want to fly!* Or, as Mark Wahlberg's character Hoitz pleads in the comedy, *The Other Guys*, "I'm a peacock, you gotta let me fly!" Ironically, although the big birds can fly, it's not very high or very far. *Awkward*. Maybe that's the only type of flying I'm going to get on this side of heaven? And maybe that's the bird I resemble to God if he ever chuckles at my impatience.

Redemption looks different for every soul, just as repentance does – and just as destruction did. The thief has an awful lot of tricks up his sleeve useful for stealing, killing, and destroying (John 10:10). Yet one reason God is God is that he can never be outwitted by the adversary. He has plans that we cannot begin to understand (Isaiah 55:9) and plans that can bring good out of what others do to harm us (Genesis 50:20). Paul puts it like this: *God can do anything, you know—far more than you could ever imagine or guess or request in your wildest dreams!* (Ephesians 3:20 MSG).

But despite God's greatness and willingness to rescue and redeem every hard thing that has ever happened in this world, there is actually something we do to start the flow of redemption to our own story: We acknowledge we have no idea how to get from point A to point B, and we finally trust *God does.*

We attach all sorts of emotional, mental and spiritual baggage to words like "sin" and "repentance." Those words instantly shut down those of us trying to protect our hearts behind walls of perfection (nothing is wrong here!), being right (if I make a mistake, I'll lose face), or just being tough (stop judging me, you hypocrite!). But the word *sin* is an ancient archer's term that means missing the bullseye, and the word *repentance* simply means turning around. An examination of the Old Testament King James language will show you that even God is said to repent of his plans.

Take the negative connotations away from those words and begin to understand that you, like an archer, are sending your arrows; your thoughts, words, and actions toward that perfection you claim to love so well. Sometimes you hit, sometimes you miss. The only shame in it all is if you throw your bow down in a tantrum because you can't hit it all the time. You can't be perfect, get over it! Examine your methods and stop blaming your bow or the tilt of the earth (or God, who makes it so hard!).

Examine not just your methods – analyze who it is that taught you how to shoot. In order to truly understand where the bullseye is, we have to choose whose idea of perfection we will ascribe to. I have learned to turn to God and what he says as my standard. Trusting God's explanations ensures that I am turned the right direction when I let my arrows fly. And when they miss, I don't have to be ashamed and turn away from God, believing I am unwanted. I turn toward God, examine the instructions again, and try anew. God has wired us with a capacity to learn and grow, and part of that growth, in his eyes, is turning around and trying again.

> *God is educating you; that's why you must never drop out. He's treating you as dear children. This trouble you're in isn't punishment; it's training, the normal experience of children. Only irresponsible parents leave children to fend for themselves. Would you prefer an irresponsible God?* (Hebrews 12:7-8 MSG)

For me, redemption looks like no longer spinning as hard as I can to make it all come out right. That is God's job. I am written into his story; I have work to do that he planned for me (Ephesians 2:10), but that work does not include being my own redeemer.

MISTAKES BELONG IN SONGS LIKE LONELY, OPEN SPACES

The story of Joseph (Genesis 37, 39-45) became for me a song in the night. I had dreams and passions that I didn't know how to use. I found myself in a pit not of my own making, then enslaved, then filled with hope, then wrongfully accused, then imprisoned, and finally face-to-face with the abuser. In the waiting and silence, I learned to trust that what others meant for evil, God would use for good. All my mistakes were being woven into the symphony of the master songwriter. There were open spaces where their pain lingered, but the music didn't stop there any longer. It went on.

The gift of redemption started with the *gift of repentance*, for it was the kindness of God that led me to repentance (Romans 2:4). I came back at age 43, broken of all my own strategies for getting life and love apart from God, and found only kindness.

Repentance looked like becoming willing to wait for redemption, learning some patience, being still, stopping the spin. As the years went by, it included an eagerness and trust that, when something bad happened and I trusted it to him, God would go to work and fight battles for me, and the outcomes would be so much better than I imagined. Redemption looked like learning to listen for his voice and only his, even in the dark or chaos, refusing the temptation to light my own fires (Is. 50:10-11). Redemption looked like praying for help, then moving ahead in faith; not just reacting in my flesh, according to my own wits. Redemption looked like starting to heal from betrayal, abandonment, and abuse. It looked like letting myself cry over the losses, like an older woman hugging a little girl who'd gotten lost, welcoming her back home. It looked like me, finally waiting for a man to open the door – not because I couldn't, but because I believed what God had said about me: I had worth and value and didn't need to prove it.

MELODY

Finally, redemption dawned in the form of an intimate relationship with Fred.

I had promised not to bug God about remarriage. If he never brought another man into my life, I had to be willing to trust him in that. But I had a longing in my heart for close companionship as I walked this broken road and a nagging sense that I couldn't heal as completely without it. *What was broken in relationship must be healed in relationship*, Sandy Burdick and *OHM* had taught me all those years before. I had a vision for what marriage could look like and friends and family members who lived good marriage out in front of me. These couples gave me hope for something better.

When the girls' dad got married again right away, they were concerned I would do the same. I reassured them not to worry; I hoped to be married again someday, but it wasn't going to happen any time soon. I felt they needed to know for their sakes that I believed in marriage. I told them if God were going to work that miracle, we would all three know when it was the right time and the right man. Conventional wisdom says that kids should never be asked when it comes to matters of marriage, but I had seen the damage done when new spouses and/or step-siblings were just dropped on children and I didn't want to make that mistake again. I didn't give them veto power, but I did let them know they had a voice and would be important to the process. I believed God would help us find someone who would be a blessing to each of us.

In 2010, I became a member of e-Harmony and the results were frustrating to say the least! Maybe I was getting out ahead of God, I thought, and let my membership expire. But I tried again, and also spent time on another Christian dating app, meeting people, having conversations, but consistently turned off by the words people used to describe themselves and their requirements for their new relationship. I had given up so much to be what everyone else wanted, and it felt like a giant step backwards to 'market' myself on the chance someone would check me out. A few times, I caught other members in lies and scams, and that was the biggest turnoff of all. I finally stopped reaching out to others, and just prayed that God would do the reaching.

In February 2011, a few days before my 50th birthday, this guy named Fred Clemens started a conversation with me on e-Harmony. Turns out it was his second day of membership and I was the second profile he viewed. One thing he was drawn by was that I was willing, rather than bash my ex, to say what I had learned from him. What had been good.

Fred and I shared many similarities and got past the *must haves* and *can't stands* pretty quickly. We moved to email correspondence and I learned he was of Mennonite heritage, just as my mother's family had been. In fact, his grandfather had been a pastor, drawn by lot, even as my own had been. As the emails flew, I appreciated the time he took to write, his spiritual depth, and the encouraging things he said. We talked openly about our stories of marriage and loss, and I talked a little about my brokenness from childhood. We had both experienced vocational loss as well, learning to trust God through hard times. He had raised three children on his own after his divorce and had been single for 20 years.

Finally, we met and his first words to me were, "I am such a goof," after driving past our designated restaurant a couple of times before finding it. I found his humility refreshing after all the posturing I saw in the online dating world, and we went from our original lunch date to a dinner date before we said goodnight.

We lived about 60 miles apart, so the letter writing continued, and the phone calls began. He asked for one of my *Secret Closet* CDs, taking it with him on a road trip a few weeks later, literally listening to it all the way there and home. Believe me, when you're a songwriter and someone starts to quote your lyrics to you, it's a very sweet thing, and that's just what he did. One time we sat and listened to it together, and I remember him just laying his head back and saying "ohhhh" every so often. It's just the sort of thing you imagine in your dreams. A publishing company exec or an artist listening to your song with total concentration. I've never had a publishing exec or artist listen like that, but this man was! He was learning my heart, and he was letting me inside his too.

We've often said that our level of trust was the most precious thing about our relationship. It flowed out of our faith journey first, but we built on that foundation, keeping our word to each other, listening deeply, practicing kindness.

I saw in Fred the most unusual ability to change. He wasn't stuck in his ways so much he couldn't also learn new things. He took everything I said into consideration; I didn't have to beg or plead for him to hear me. Part of that was probably my own healing; recovering the truth that my voice counted. But part of it was just being around a safe man who listened well and cared deeply. Instead of repeating the distance dance, Fred and I were finding new steps toward healthy, authentic relationship.

He began attending the same recovery ministry I had been part of for years and learning more about how his own childhood had impacted his life. A shared language from the *Open Hearts Ministry* curriculum made our conversations even richer.

One of the first things we did as we got more serious was attend a conference on remarriage and stepparenting. Again, I appreciated that he would take time to wade into these waters, rather than adopting a bravado that it was unnecessary, or thinking it should be saved for if we got engaged.

His transparency continued; his humility continued. Never once did he use a critical word about his ex, despite the fact that she had basically abandoned their marriage before the divorce. His children are delightful, and as I've gotten to know them over the years, they've helped redeem the losses I felt in my previous stepparenting journey. Fred also learned to know and love my girls and even through tough moments in each of our lives, he has remained steady.

We shared self-deprecating humor, and both loved a good pun. Unfortunately, Fred even loved a bad pun. Fortunately, I was already in love with him when I realized that!

Certainly, we have a lot of differences, and there's nothing like the years flying by to reveal those. He is a computer programmer and historian. He likes to wake up at least two to three hours before work and take his time getting ready, then he's steady at it from dawn to dusk. I'm a left-handed, right brained, slightly introverted, intuitive, feeling, perceiver (INFP, for those who follow such things!) and began to value history only after I became historic. I like to roll out of bed and go straight to work, full of zeal for about 5 hours. Then I like a nap.

At one point in our courtship, we broke up. There were dynamics and habits that needed attending to, but no movement. Rather than continue forward, we went our separate ways. Over the course of the next seven months, several things happened that brought us back together, and we are both grateful for the experience of not moving further toward marriage, blindly hoping for change.

Fred set in motion some important changes even though there was no promise of a future between us; and he also had a few dates with others, as did I. Ironically, those dates helped draw us back together. I begin to viscerally miss the depth and kindness Fred brought to my life. I could see ever more clearly that the safety of our relationship was a rare and precious thing. It was terrifying for me to enter into covenantal relationship again and I had to accept the ways we were wired differently, recognizing that conflict and compromise would be essential to marriage. On his part, dating another helped him clarify what he wanted, and what he had seen in ours.

When we decided to date again, it seemed only a formality as we moved toward marriage. It was late April; we were engaged in June and married in October 2013.

I walked down the aisle toward Fred, one daughter on each of my arms, to *Bless the Broken Road*. Each one of our children participated in the ceremony by placing a unique plant they had chosen into the soil of a planter Fred and I prepared. It looked rather messy, like our lives, but we were committing to nourishing and loving that happy mess of unique plants. Our courtship wasn't perfect; our families weren't perfect – but we were letting our arrows fly in the right direction and there was joy in all of our hearts that day. I trust and pray that this big God of redemption will continue the work he's started in our family as well as our individual lives.

We are every bit as much in love today as we were when we married; maybe more so on my part because the years have revealed more of his commitment to me, and more of his trustworthiness. We've been through many trying circumstances: job loss for him and vocational wanderings for me, two cross-country moves, the sale of two homes, the purchase of two homes, plus two apartment homes as he went to take jobs before I could join him. So two separations due to new jobs. I've lost both my parents and one of my siblings and was the executor for my siblings' estate – all wearying and wearing to the soul but made less so by so many dear friends, family, and a spouse walking the broken road with me.

Today, after so much anguish, we agree the lines have fallen for us in pleasant places (Psalm 16:6). With each year I can see more clearly what Fred seemed to know from almost the beginning. God brought us together. Melody was resurrecting hearts that evil sought to destroy.

Through it all, our foundation of trust has been rocked, but never cracked. We have made it a habit to have the hard conversations as well as the easy and fun ones. It is an unequivocal blessing, given my history, to be able to have a hard conversation, even open conflict, without fear of abandonment, betrayal, or some type of abuse. We have made it a habit to pray about everything, and since the early days of our relationship, prayer has played a foundational role. To have someone warring beside you in the battle, not opposing you – this is redemption!

We've now welcomed five grandchildren (from his kids) into our blended family, and we are truly blended, racially, ethnically, and culturally. It makes for some interesting holidays and storytelling, not to mention beautiful babies!

When you've been through so much disruption in your life, it's not easy to trust God, yourself, others, or a spouse. It's not easy to comprehend joy, especially if you kept a childhood vow to always smile through pain for about four decades. Such healing will likely take a lifetime, but if I stop and look back at how far I've come, I find reasons to trust and hope for good things to come. God did amazing things when I finally ran to him, broken of my own ways.

I'm no longer a flickering wick or a bruised reed, and isn't that gospel news? Psalm 131 from *The Message* is a beautiful lyric to describe where I'm at today with redemption:

> *God, I'm not trying to rule the roost,*
> *I don't want to be king of the mountain.*
> *I haven't meddled where I have no business*
> *or fantasized grandiose plans.*
> *I've kept my feet on the ground,*
> *I've cultivated a quiet heart.*
> *Like a baby content in its mother's arms,*
> *my soul is a baby content.*
> *Wait, Israel, for God. Wait with hope.*
> *Hope now; hope always!*

Today, repentance looks like me practicing honesty at my computer rather than spinning for love or acceptance. Telling you the story of a girl who pretended to never have a need when her life was shattered. She hated showing pain so thoroughly she skied down a mountain with a torn anterior cruciate ligament. In her repentance, she has now writ large her mistakes and sin, her desperate need and brokenness, her longings and pain. No more spinning. No more the driving need to impress, just a growing desire to do whatever it is God wants her to do, and a trust that is firm.

God has shown me that he doesn't need big, extravagant gestures. What he wants most is a willing heart; a humble heart not out to prove anything to the world. A trusting heart, one who leans into him for strength rather than trying to do it in self's power. A listening heart, ear to the wind of the Spirit, ready to move when God wants to take me a way that seems foolish to the world.

Perhaps I'll never fly – or perhaps I'm already flying and just can't feel it because I'm held by a savior for whom falling is just flying. To my eyes, I'm just walking on, keeping my feet on the ground as the Psalmist says. I'm falling less often but am also less concerned with public image and more concerned with that audience of one. The song he is singing over me erases the pain of the past with a redemption I could have never imagined or achieved on my own. My mistakes are being woven into his symphony, and the song is not complete yet.

Chapter 13: What Does Redemption Look Like?
QUESTIONS FOR REFLECTION

Question: If redemption begins with repentance, which means to turn the other way (toward God rather than away from God), have you had important moments of turning in your life? If so, how does repentance for you differ from repentance for another? If not, what keeps you from it?

Question: Whose voice is loudest in your head, telling you how you do things wrong, criticizing your every move, causing you to want to quit learning something? Can you distinguish that voice from the voice of God?

Question: What is necessary for you to fear God – as in respect God, without being afraid of God?

Question: What is necessary for you to trust God to bring something good out of anything bad that's happened to you? To weave any mistake you've made into his symphony?

Action: After you've been hurt, the easiest thing is to never trust again, to isolate and construct a life free of relational risk. But it rarely works that way and, furthermore, God wired us for relationship! Your action step for this chapter is to take what you've learned about safe relationships and practice one step toward being a safe person yourself, one step toward God and one step toward another human.

Sea of glass, brokenness
Cut you too 'til life was death
Savior kind, you bled and died
At hands you loved and lips that lied

Your sea of glass and brokenness
Was colored by the stain of this:
All sin upon the Holy Son –
The perfect one has stain become.

Yet love so great it saw beyond
The sea of glass, the brokenness
And from it forged a window paned
With fragments of the crime, the shame

And through its beauty, through this frame
We see your love and may the same be seen in us…
Sea of glass, brokenness
A window stained and aptly named
Forgiveness.

February 2005

Chapter 14
Preparing the Heart to Offer Forgiveness

I'll freely admit that forgiveness is something I struggle with, whether of self or others. But maybe I'm in good company. I know very few people who sail through the unavoidable abandonments, betrayals, and losses of life without collecting some baggage. Thing is, I also know people who let that baggage become their furniture, and then the walls of their fortresses. They have plenty of suitcases packed and are ready to retreat (or attack) at the hint of strife. That's not me anymore, gratefully.

My friend Mark Bonham, at the time executive director of *OHM*, said something like, "It doesn't matter whether you got run over by a Mack truck or a moped, you're the one who got hurt, and you're the one who has to heal."

In other words, the driver who hit me isn't the one who has to undergo surgery, or intense physical therapy. The driver isn't the one who has to forgive. That's me (although it certainly helps if the driver feels remorse and comes back to help).

Sometimes it feels like I've been hit by a lengthy caravan. I no sooner think it's done, and a camel steps on me. I'm certain a few of you relate. But I'll also admit, that just like trying to work out my childhood trauma in marriage, I have tended to land in places where I am reminded of past pain, and running has been my kneejerk response. Avoiding hard places and hard conversations isn't the way to healing, but it might be evidence that true, full healing hasn't yet been completed. So, I am on my way, but in keeping with the metaphor that flows through this book, I might be limping toward forgiveness when I'd rather fly. I'm far from a perfect example (like Jesus, who with his dying breath was able to ask God to forgive those who killed him), but I've learned a few things along the way that bear reflection.

WATCHING OVER YOUR HEART

There's a deep chasm between forgiveness and reconciliation. And, just as deep is the chasm between forgiveness and letting yourself be run over again if you can stop it. They both have to do with something I've talked about before: naivete vs. wisdom. A verse I'd memorized in childhood became more than pretty words in my forties: "Watch over your heart with all diligence, For from it flow the springs of life. (Proverbs 4:23 NASB)." Don't be naïve! Be wise!

I penned these evocative words in 2007: *So how do I watch over this river I can't see / That flows with his life in and out of me? / Oh it's clear this is a treasure he's given me to guard / But I have been so reckless in matters of my heart.*

The question was more salient to the rest of my life and story than I knew as I began to heal. You may wonder what watching over your heart has to do with forgiveness, but it has everything to do with where life comes from, and certainly the issues of forgiveness and unforgiveness can be life-giving or life-sapping. Unfortunately, we can't just wake up one day and say "Heal, heart of mine! Forgive!" It is a process, much like recovery from being run over, only perhaps harder because the wounds are not as evident as broken bones and lacerated flesh.

CHEAP FORGIVENESS

Even as a child I practiced a type of forgiveness toward my abuser, and as I grew up, I just went on in that manner, pretending pain didn't really hurt, offering a smile rather than the truth. I had to devalue my heart to get to that place. I had to teach my heart to be silent, rather than listen to its cries for help; to be dishonest rather than offer a raw truth that might hurt someone and my relationship with them. This is what I call "cheap forgiveness," and it is cheap because we don't have to count the cost. True forgiveness can only be offered if you have looked honestly at the damage, and that's as true for the one hurt as the one who does the offending. If you're going to speak the truth about damage, you must first believe there was something *good* to even become damaged.

As I look back, I think the first step toward real forgiveness was believing that, even though I had in many ways hated and disregarded my own heart, God didn't and hadn't. I had to trust that God saw something good that he had woven into me when he knit me together in my mother's womb (Psalm 139:13), and that whatever he saw was wound up with his plans and purposes for my life. It was worth guarding, not recklessly throwing around, like pearls to pigs (Matthew 7:6). My acknowledgement of self-worth had nothing to do with being pretty enough, smart enough, or confident of my worldly abilities. It had to do with trusting what God has said, rather than putting my confidence in what others said or believed about me.

A story about Jesus and Peter was of great encouragement during this process. Peter was as rascally a rabbit as there ever was, constantly doing and saying things that were out of place – things for which he was often reprimanded by Jesus. Nevertheless, when Jesus first laid eyes on him his name was *Simon*. And before Simon could do a single thing or utter a single word, Jesus changed his name to Peter, meaning "rock (Jn. 1:42)." That's the thing about Jesus. He has eyes that see beneath your exterior, your damage, your baggage, your intentions. He sees what he wove into you even before birth, and he will call it out in you just like he did Peter, if you let him. It was Peter who much later said, "love covers over a multitude of sins (1 Pet. 4:8 NIV)," and I believe he spoke from direct experience. That gives me hope; maybe it will you too.

A friend and I also did a study called *The Search for Significance* by Robert McGee and I commend it to you if this is an area of struggle. It goes through Scripture after Scripture, revealing the way God sees us compared to the way we get bent and twisted in reaction to our vulnerabilities and pain. It began a deeper healing that was preparing the way for the next step.

Forgiving myself has been a big part of my journey. Initially, owning the truth that the abuse wasn't my idea and wasn't my fault was the key to more grace for my own story and self. But I had grown up with a harsh critic inside, always whipping me into shape so I could look good to others. That tendency didn't change overnight and still rears its ugly head when something goes wrong. I've had grace for the little girl, but not so much for the woman who made so many mistakes and encountered so many losses.

Knowing my God-given value helped me stop running and start facing the pain. The suitcases that surrounded me like a fortress were slowly emptied, and finally removed, as I began to name and share the stories of my life in safe small groups and with safe friends. Shame or the fear of shame didn't have the power over me it once did. I could watch over my heart with God's help because I valued its Maker and his good work, instead of practicing the hypervigilance I had lived with for so long – the strategy that had failed to protect me anyway.

OWNING THE TRUTH

The next step was owning the truth about others. This was hard for me because I was a Pollyanna, making my way through life by smiling and spinning, thinking mostly about my impression on others. I had to stop all that in order to even see others, look into their eyes and into their behaviors, become okay with judging character and saying *no* to close relationship with those who weren't committed to the honesty, authenticity and integrity that governed my own behavior. We are schooled this day and age that judgment is politically incorrect, but the truth is every single person on planet earth is constantly making judgments. It's part of our wiring to draw conclusions about others, and shutting that ability down is one way of *not* guarding our hearts. This doesn't give me the right to judge others spiritually, to act in critical, judgmental, superior ways toward people I don't agree with, or to believe they are somehow worthless. Never. All I have to do is remember how Jesus changed Peter's name the moment he saw him to know that. Only someone who sees like that can make spiritual judgments. What I can do is watch over what and who comes and goes into my own heart, making room for the living water of God to pour in and pour out without all my old filtering devices, baggage, and perfectionism getting in the way.

The story from Scripture that really coalesced the chasm between forgiveness and reconciliation for me was

Joseph's testing of his half-brothers before revealing who he was (Genesis 42-45). Obviously, somewhere along his perilous journey from being thrown in a pit and left to die by them, to being sold into slavery in a foreign land, to unjust accusations, prison, and forgotten promises, Joseph's heart became open to forgiveness rather than becoming entrenched in bitterness. Otherwise, when he sees them again (Genesis 42:8-10), he might have cursed them, sent them away ashamed and starving, or even had them killed. Certainly he had the power to take vengeance. Perhaps this is why it can be a long journey from abuse to forgiveness: It takes time to get your heart ready to forgive rather than seek vengeance; it takes time for God to work out his purposes in your life through the damage and trauma of childhood wounds. Time for you to be able to learn and believe, like Joseph, "You planned evil against me but God used those same plans for my good...(Genesis 50:20 MSG)."

Regardless, this story gave me permission to test another's heart. To not be naïve when it came to forgiveness, offering cheap words like, "It's okay, I'm sure you didn't mean to hurt me," or "Oh, it's fine, I've been through worse." As I've said before, that only teaches people that I can be used or hurt without consequence. Joseph didn't make that mistake. He knew the very things that would elicit the truth from his estranged family, and he needed to hear the truth. Did they regret their decisions that fateful day so long ago? Did they even remember him? Did they treat his younger brother Benjamin in the same way? So, without revealing his whole heart (he cried but won't allow them to see it), he tested their motives and hearts over a period of months. Once he saw they were sorry *and* honest *and* willing to sacrifice themselves for the sake of others, he could reveal his identity and his vulnerable heart of forgiveness (and in fact this time he wept openly before them – so loudly that the house staff hears. Gen. 45:1-2) and reconciliation began.

That's a happy ending to a hard story.

It is not as happy to test another and find they are not truly repentant because then you must continue to keep your heart open to forgiveness when you know full reconciliation is not possible. Joseph had to live in that tension for many years before famine drove his abusers to him, and then for the months it took for him to test and trust the changes in their character.

In my own story of childhood abuse, my abuser said he was sorry and even paid for counselling. He admitted to my parents what had happened. We had a phone conversation where we talked through the scenes of abuse because I wanted to be certain we remembered the same things. But I never really shared with him the pain and havoc his abuse caused in my life, and at that point, I don't think I even fully understood it yet. Of course, he could see some of that havoc, and I was willing to let it go at that. You see, I didn't fully trust him because he still said things that hurt me, and when he asked me to sign a letter stating I would never bring charges against him in court, I saw that he really didn't trust me either. He didn't want to know my heart or build trust with me, just to close his own suitcase on the past. And I was still too afraid of conflict and further damage to move in closer. Before I was ready, he died, and the chance for more reconciliation passed by. After his memorial service, one of his closest friends revealed that my abuser had talked to her about his regret, calling it "the blackest mark on his life," telling her how much he loved me and grieved over his actions. And through words spoken at his funeral, I learned more about him as a man I didn't know, not shadowed so deeply by my own experience. That has helped my healing too, but I still regret that total reconciliation never happened. Perhaps one day it will – and wouldn't that be a happy ending to a hard story?

Aside from my childhood abuser, I continue to struggle to forgive people who've harmed me, so I continue to seek God's help and mercy in getting my heart ready to extend grace and pray that the day to offer it will arrive.

HOW DOES GOD FORGIVE?

Do you believe God forgives just because someone says the right words in the right sequence, like a chant or mantra? I don't think so, and if we are to follow his example, we need to explore the question of how and when God forgives. If you try to understand God's heart around the issue, you'll get a bigger picture of one who loves "mercy, not sacrifice (Hosea 6:6, Matthew 9:13)" and the knowledge of God rather than burnt offerings. (Hosea 6:6 ESV)," God bends toward mercy and wants to be known. He is not moved by rituals or rhetoric. You can't con God with fancy words or whipped up performance, and you can't buy his forgiveness by any sort of sacrifice save one: The sacrifices of God are a broken spirit; a broken and contrite heart... (Psalm 51:17 ESV)." Paul teaches that there are even two different types of grief, one that leads nowhere because the sorrow flows out of getting caught, and another that leads to repentance, life, and no regret: "For godly grief produces a repentance that leads to salvation without regret, whereas worldly grief produces death (2 Corinthians 7:10 ESV)."

But what could be more important than hearing what God says about himself? I would certainly want to let you tell me about yourself if we were getting acquainted. When asked to show his glory to Moses, God talks about his character while only showing Moses his back, and how he describes himself says volumes: "The LORD, the LORD, the compassionate and gracious God, slow to anger, abounding in love and faithfulness, maintaining love to thousands, and forgiving wickedness, rebellion and sin. Yet he does not leave the guilty unpunished... (Exodus 34:6-7

NIV)." So, God is loving, gracious, and forgiving – but not to those who haven't realized their need for forgiveness! They are considered "guilty" in his eyes.

Isaiah, probably the most important prophet in the Old Testament, is commissioned directly *by* God to speak *for* God, and among the first words he speaks on behalf of God, says:

> *When you spread out your hands in prayer, I hide my eyes from you; even when you offer many prayers, I am not listening. Your hands are full of blood! Wash and make yourselves clean. Take your evil deeds out of my sight; stop doing wrong. Learn to do right; seek justice. Defend the oppressed. Take up the cause of the fatherless; plead the case of the widow.* (Isaiah 1:15-17 NIV)

In other words, *I can't hear you because your guilt is blocking the communication between us.* Trying to forgive those who've sinned against us before they admit their guilt and demonstrate their sorrow is trying to be "godlier" than even God! John the Baptizer teaches, "bear fruit in keeping with repentance (Matthew 3:8 ESV)," and from David's great song of confession, we learn "a broken and contrite heart you, God, will not despise (Psalm 51:17 NIV)." That's true of us in our relationships as well. When an abuser shows you their brokenness over their actions, and you can see good, healthy fruit resulting from their new way of seeing things, trust me, if your heart has been prepared, forgiveness won't feel so hard.

So, what about the most heinous criminal (or us) who has an epiphany about what they've done and comes to a place of healthy respect for God as the one who can forgive? David, who experienced God's forgiveness for murder and adultery, says:

> *For his unfailing love toward those who fear him is as great as the height of the heavens above the earth. He has removed our sins as far from us as the*

east is from the west. The Lord is like a father to his children, tender and compassionate to those who fear him. For he knows how weak we are; he remembers we are only dust. (Psalm 103:11-14 NLT)

The Psalms also proclaim, "If you, O Lord, should mark iniquities, O Lord, who could stand? But with you there is forgiveness, that you may be feared. (Psalm 130:3-4 ESV)." God is not just willing, but eager to forgive, and when our hearts align with his over how we have wronged others or been wronged. *When we appropriately fear God,* the process can start.

ASK FOR HELP FROM THE ONE WHO KNOWS THE WHOLE TRUTH

Man looks at the outside, but God looks at the heart (1 Samuel 16:7), and while we cannot see others' hearts like God the Father, Son or Holy Spirit, we can ask for help as we listen for the hearts of others by asking good questions that are part of the process of forgiveness. What questions would you like to ask one who has hurt you, betrayed your trust, or wounded your ability to trust again? What restitution could they make that would help you trust they were, in fact, repentant? Abusers are skilled at side-stepping responsibility, transferring it all back to you. But if an abuser or one who wounded you came to you, repentant, how could you be prepared for the conversation? How can you get your heart ready for forgiveness, and what would be necessary for complete reconciliation?

These are ways in which you can examine yourself, and ask God for help, even if the conversation with one who wounded you is a long time off, or never happens.

Being open to forgiveness is making sure your heart is ready – it is not offering forgiveness and reconciliation before an admission of guilt and just because the words, "I'm sorry" are uttered. This is something I believe we have expected of ourselves at the peril of honesty and integrity, not to mention the peril of making ourselves vulnerable to dangerous people whose intentions are *not* good. People can say, "I'm sorry," because they got caught or just want everything to go back to the way it was. In Jesus' oft-quoted words to Peter (Matthew 18:21-22 NLT), he says you must forgive seventy times seven (or some versions read 77 times). But look at the context: Jesus' words to Peter are set between how to deal with someone who has offended you by confronting them (vs. 15-17), and Jesus' parable of the unforgiving debtor (vs. 23-35). In the first situation, you confront injury, taking others with you if necessary (vs. 15-17). If the offender doesn't admit guilt, you need to let them go (v. 18), even cut off contact. In the second situation Jesus teaches that the key to having God's grace for your own sin is forgiving those *who beg forgiveness of you.*

In short, if someone hurts you and doesn't ask forgiveness, see verses 15-18, but if they own their offense and seek your forgiveness, see verses 23-35. What Jesus faults is the failure to forgive due to a stingy, uncompromising, selfish manner: Someone begged forgiveness and it was withheld, even though the one who is begged has himself been a beggar who received grace. When a *repentant* person asks pardon, we must forgive – seventy times seven.

When someone admits to wronging us, we should take it seriously, not rush past it in an effort for reconciliation (or vengeance), which sometimes we do simply to relieve the tension of the moment. Living in tension is something we're not good at; letting one who's hurt us see our heart and asking to see theirs too is something we're not skilled in. We'd much rather shuffle our feet and mutter, "okay," then walk away, still holding on to our wounds. I'm not talking here about someone spilling your coffee and saying, "I'm sorry." I'm not asking you to elongate into an ordeal those little, everyday irritations that happen to us all. I'm talking about the conversation that can happen when someone you are in relationship with rolls over a boundary and hurts you, or worse. Set aside time yourself or with a trusted advisor to explore the offense and what it has truly cost you and be ready to offer those truths to the offender when you talk. If you are talking to someone who has abused or traumatized you, meet them with a trusted third party who is able to keep the table safe and process what happened with you afterwards. If your offender is not willing for this kind of safe conversation, there's every chance that they are not truly repentant. Ask a few questions that clarify what they've done to hurt the relationship and how they feel about it. Is the offense they are asking forgiveness for the same thing you are grieving? If not, be prepared to clarify, offer the truth, and listen again. If they are repentant and you can offer forgiveness under these circumstances it will mean more and do more to heal you and the relationship than you know.

REVOKING REVENGE

Once I began to value my heart and life like God did, and see myself and others honestly, I could go to work on something known as "revoking revenge." That simply means giving up the idea of getting even with those who've harmed me. And *that* means trusting that God will do a better job of revenge than I. "It is mine to avenge; I will repay (Deuteronomy 32:35 NIV)," says God.

Whether you've found protection in anger (and your walls of protection are covered with thorns for pricking anyone who tries to get close), or you've found protection in lying dormant like a rug under another's feet, taking the hits so you don't have to confront anyone, you'll find it hard to lay down your "right" to revenge for the ways you've gotten hurt. Sometimes we employ different strategies with different people, using any means at hand to get even and protect ourselves from further hurt. It doesn't matter what your strategies have been, they are ways of coping you developed pursing a type of self-protection that hurts in the end. Revoking revenge means you must trust that another, God, has your back. Lay down your weapons, and especially if you find yourself hurting innocent people caught in the crossfire. Not easy – but freeing in the end. I'm not suggesting you give up safety! Just give up revenge. It's a step toward making your heart ready to forgive.

It's important to recognize that Jesus also taught our willingness to forgive others is tied to God's forgiveness of us. I hear it in the prayer he used as an example with his disciples (Matthew 6:12 NLT), "forgive us our sins, as we have forgiven those who sin against us." I hear it in his parable about the servant who was forgiven so much but refused to forgive the one who owed him a much smaller debt (Matthew 18:35). It is God's way to forgive our debts and trespasses, and it has to be ours too. If you are truly willing to revoke revenge, and you do the work of preparing your heart to forgive, God will forgive you when you repent of your own strategies to find life and safety apart from him. Nowhere does Jesus suggest that we owe it to people to forgive them if they don't concede their need and wrong. He does teach us to pray for our enemies, and he does say that God will forgive us as we forgive others – tightfistedly or openhandedly. It's worth doing the work.

WHERE I'M AT

So, in the tension of having been forgiven much and struggling to forgive in a wholehearted way, I live. I wrestle to soften my heart toward those who've hurt me and never seemed to be sorry for it; those who've lived smugly in their sense of superiority and sacrificed me in the process. I've realized God is so much bigger and his strategies for convicting them of wrongdoing (and me too!) are so much more creative than my own. I've revoked revenge and turn them over to God whenever I start to obsess on what happened. I believe my job is to be ready to forgive as far as it is within my power to be. If I ever hear an "I'm sorry," I want to be ready to ask good questions, test repentance, and offer forgiveness. Hopefully reconciliation will follow. What I never want to do is reject that "I'm sorry," in favor of holding my own victimization or vengeance over their head. I want to let go and be free. I dream of heaven, where there are no wrongs and every heart is totally free to love without fear of vulnerability. To that end, I work.

PERMISSION TO FAIL

Finally, it's important that we give ourselves permission to fail. Perfectionism isn't a Godly characteristic – it's a restless drivenness that makes us unsatisfied at every turn, haunted by something just beyond our grasp. As a reformed perfectionist, I can see how my actions flowed out of my pain, trying to never get it wrong again so I wouldn't get hurt or be exposed or feel shame. Give yourself permission to fail at your movement toward honesty, authenticity, and forgiveness, and ask safe others to offer grace to you as well. Just keep moving! Sometimes, practice without criticism (self- or other) is what we need to begin feeling comfortable in new ways of thinking and acting. When Jesus says, "be perfect, therefore, as your heavenly Father is perfect (Matthew 5:48)," those words can and have been translated as "be complete," or "be mature" from the Greek word "téleios." Both are concepts we would still be unable to reach *perfectly*, but it feels better to aim at a more realistic target. The Amplified translation reads, "growing into spiritual maturity both in mind and character, actively integrating godly values into your daily life." That's something we *can* definitely do.

Being whole or mature leaves room for the imperfection of humans. Whole people still make mistakes and have regrets – for which they ask forgiveness. They work and go to worship with imperfect people without harshly judging or criticizing every action. They live with imperfect spouses and children without controlling and manipulating to make everything look good on the outside when the inside is crumbling. Whole people are mature, and especially when they are lovers of God, you can viscerally feel their love and kindness. I believe the people I have been blessed to follow in the faith have taught me something about what God is like. They've forgiven without patronizing, offered help without judgment and criticism, and accepted what I had to offer without making me feel small. They've helped me heal, and their example has helped me prepare my own heart to be generous with others.

They say you can't give away what you don't have. I entered adulthood without much of anything to give but tried to give it away for the next 20 years anyway. Finally, almost another 20 years later, I've seen God in action through men and women who have lived into the image in which they are created. Because of them, I understand more about the power of unconditional, *agape* love and forgiveness. God has promised he will complete the work started in my own life, but even short of complete, I now have something to give away.

JESUS OUR AUTHOR AND FINISHER
Hebrews 12 calls Jesus "the author and finisher of our faith," or, as the *New Living Translation* puts it, the "instigator and perfecter." When we let him, he is writing a story that is better than we could ask or imagine (Ephesians 3:20).

There is probably no one who had more to forgive than Jesus. Think about it. Not only was he abandoned by his friends and abused by his enemies in his hour of crisis, he was abandoned by his beloved Father. And worse, he knew

195

it was coming. He had to prepare his heart to do God's will, knowing all along it was God's will that he bear *all the weight* of *all the sin* of mankind, start to finish. Perhaps he could have been ready for that, but to do it all without his Father's presence? Jesus was so connected to God, he said, "the Son can do nothing by himself; he can do only what he sees his Father doing, because whatever the Father does the Son also does. (John 5:19 NIV)." But, for those moments of abandonment, he couldn't see, hear, or feel the Father. The connection was lost because God cannot be part of sin. He hung by himself, likely naked, on a cross, dying to self and dying to sin. And why? Because although he knew it had to be, he also knew the joy of *offering* forgiveness and ridding mankind of the penalty of sin. And he knew the joy that was waiting for him on the other side of the hard work (Hebrews 12:2).

I don't know about you, but my experience has taught me that if I can find something ahead of me that I know will be good, something I can look forward to, I can get through almost anything. Preparing to offer forgiveness is hard work, but the joy and relief that spreads through your soul and body when you are asked for – and can offer – authentic forgiveness can't compare. This is the joy set before us as we do our work. Jesus has promised to finish our faith too; he won't give up as he puts together all those stained and shattered pieces of glass that cut and tear at our lives. He's making a masterpiece. A stained-glass window through which we'll see our stories in the light of forgiveness.

Chapter 14: Preparing the Heart to Offer Forgiveness
QUESTIONS FOR REFLECTION

Question: Describe "cheap" forgiveness. Have you ever offered it? On the flip side, have you ever tested repentance like Joseph did before offering forgiveness?

Question: Is your heart worth *you* guarding it? If so, how do you do that correctly (i.e. without shutting it down)?

Question: What questions would you like to ask one who has hurt you, betrayed your trust, or wounded your ability to trust again? What restitution could they make that would help you trust they were, in fact, repentant?

Question: How can you get your heart ready to forgive, and what would be necessary for complete reconciliation?

Something to ponder: Would you rather have revenge or reconciliation? How hard is it to trust that God has your back, and that God's vengeance is better than yours?

Action: I've made the point that perfectionism can get in our way as we view others' wrongs or our own. Your action step now is to give yourself permission to fail as you reach toward growth in understanding and practicing forgiveness and reconciliation. You *will* fail to be perfect but keep moving toward the goal anyway. Write your permission slip below:

Long before there was this desert
You were watching over me, and
You saw the chains that bound me, and
You longed to set me free
But I turned my gaze away from love
That wouldn't be denied, so you
Wooed me to this desert
Of my desperate, broken pride

Speak tenderly, speak tenderly
There is nothing in this wilderness but you
Speak tenderly, speak tenderly
I am captured by your beauty
And my soul is satisfied
My soul is satisfied

July 2006

Chapter 15
Just Keep Walking: Encouragement for the Journey

I'd like to offer some encouragement to you on your own journey: Just keep walking.

It won't be like mine. No two people have the same faith walk, or recovery journey, or redemption story. No two people have had the same set of circumstances in their families of origin, and if they suffered the same trauma, it won't affect them the way it affected another.

That's part of what makes our Big God so incredible. He knows your history, every step of it; if you trust him, he will lead you through the narrow gate and up the narrow road that leads to life. We don't like that it's narrow because *we* don't want to be narrow, we want our lives to be expansive. Further into God's training program now, I understand he wants our lives to be full and rich and fruitful, but it's a narrow road of training that gets us ready, like an athlete preparing for a race who focuses on just a few important things. This journey will require both patience and courage of you, of that I am certain. You will *think* you're there; you will *hope* you're there. You will think the painful past should be behind you; you will long for the promises of God to be fulfilled *now*. But I'm encouraging you, don't be discouraged even when you're disappointed. There is redemption on this broken road, and the journey is often the point!

> *We are pressed on every side by troubles, but we are not crushed. We are perplexed, but not driven to despair. We are hunted down, but never abandoned by God. We get knocked down, but we are not destroyed. Through suffering, our bodies continue to share in the death of Jesus so that the life of Jesus may also be seen in our bodies.* (2 Corinthians 4:8-10 NLT)

This is the training program of trust. Its toughness can still surprise me, even as long as I've been walking. There is something about death that Jesus wants us to understand. He once said, "Truly, truly, I say to you, unless a grain of wheat falls into the earth and dies, it remains alone; but if it dies, it bears much fruit. (John 12:24) He was speaking of his own death, but he was also speaking of an eternal truth. Paul talked a lot about dying to selfish desires, and dying to sin, and dying to the law – always dying so that we could live in true freedom. I think the closer we get to freedom, the more fruit we can bear because we simply are no longer afraid of dying.

I've experienced this in my own life: a movement away from fear and into freedom. You've read my story, and you know that I lived in fear for almost all of my life before God interrupted my falling. Of all the concepts in the Christian life, freedom in Christ was the hardest to grasp. But I'm progressing, and I'm starting to think that entering freedom has a lot to do with entering the Promised Land. I'm wondering if it's more a set of truths we own than a particular destination. And I'll tell you why I'm considering that.

Even as my toes found the hot sand of the wilderness, I was expecting milk and honey, the Promised Land. Like a little kid in the back seat, I kept bugging God, "are we there yet?" But I had to recover from slavery, and it's taken a long time.

I was a slave to others' opinions and approval, and to my own desire to be perfect. The rush of shame was always waiting to flood in if I made a mistake in front of others, and of course I've done a lot of that. I had to be freed of what might be called "love addiction," a pathological need to get my sense of security and worth from another person. I had to break the chains of denial and the vow of always smiling I kept for 43 years. I had to start weeping over my very real losses and very real sin, and awaken to the desire for something better. I had to unpack all the layers covering who God made me: what I thought, what I felt, where I tried to be something I wasn't for the sake of others or for self-glory. I had to find my voice again, learn to speak into conflict, stand up for what was right and leave the outcomes to God's justice. I had to begin the hard work of preparing my heart to be ready to forgive.

There's nothing like too much sun, sand, thirst, and harsh environments day and night, for years, to help you pay attention. God speaks to unfaithful Israel (Wrestles-With-God), and me, through Hosea, "Therefore I am now going to allure her; I will lead her into the wilderness and speak tenderly to her (Hosea 2:14 NIV)." Those years in the wilderness removed all the distractions and I became able to hear the voice of God speaking tenderly. They were desert wanderings, but they were also part of my redemption.

In the story of God's deliverance of the Hebrews, you'll find God called his people out from slavery for this purpose: to make them a kingdom of priests (Exodus 19:6). A priest (thousands of years before there was such a thing as the Catholic Church) has the honor of representing God to the people, and the people to God. Imagine *every person,* man and woman, able to represent God well to those around them and also able to take the broken and hurting to the throne of grace. A serious training program, but God believed it could be done.

I am still on that journey, somewhere between slavery and priesthood, and my ideas of what the Promised Land is have changed drastically, even in the last year.

WHERE IS *MY* PROMISED LAND?

Throughout my story, I've mentioned multiple times that a new level of understanding, of healing, of deliverance brought me one step closer to the Promised Land, and it's true. But it all got a clearer still on January 1, 2019 as I sat in my living room, Bible in lap, and listened for God's voice. What I heard that day started a shaking in my life, and it hasn't stopped yet.

The Promised Land has been my coveted destination practically all my life. In recovery, I've gotten much more honest about where I've been and where I am. I've stopped pretending and learned to enjoy walking when I'd rather fly. But this quiet time on the cusp of a new year helped me get honest about *where I'm going.* I wanted direction for the year ahead, and during prayer, unbidden, a Scripture reference floated up for me.

Sadly, I was pretty sure what it said:

> *Have I not commanded you? Be strong and courageous. Do not be afraid; do not be discouraged, for the Lord your God will be with you wherever you go.* (Joshua 1:9 NIV)

Sure enough, there it was in black and white. God wanted me to be strong and courageous – again! I felt frustrated. *When is it going to be my turn to enter the Promised Land, God? That place where everything goes well for me; where I get to soar like I believe I should; where I can lay down my armor and not need such strength and courage?*

Even as a little kid, hearing Bible stories at my Mom's knee, I had heard the story of the "land flowing with milk and honey" promised to Moses at the burning bush. God wanted to deliver his special people from slavery, and this was how the land he would take them to was described over and over in the Old Testament. It seemed a promise worth pursuing!

And that's when the Lord hit me, and hit me good with truth. The Promised Land was rich and beautiful – yes, but the majority of what happened there could be characterized as spiritual and literal *warfare*. I read on in Joshua, realizing more fully all the reasons that man needed strength and courage. I wondered how many times he had to look back to God's commissioning of his ministry in order to find the strength to go on? How many times did he regret the mantle of leadership that belonged to him? How many times did he need to put behind him what others would say, choosing instead to hang on every word from the mouth of God (Deuteronomy 8:3)?

Flowing with milk and honey brings up visions of rest and fullness. And there has been that too, but compare it to a night in a beautiful bed and breakfast rather than a camp out at a lush buffet, open 24-7-365. While it's true that God is intimately involved in fighting the battles his people face, they have always done their fair share of warfare. They must take the land, then protect the land. They must nurture faith and faithfulness. This is as true of us in the battles we fight for freedom as it was for the ancient Hebrews.

God also showed me several astonishing truths during the previous year as I wrote a month-long set of devotions called "Light in the Darkness" for *Words of Hope*.

Did you realize that the Israelites had to walk all day *and then all night* to get to the Red Sea? I always imagined the pillar of fire by night to be a sort of giant nightlight, while everyone rolled out mats and laid down – kind of like kindergarten. But, there's this:

> *And the Lord went before them by day in a pillar of cloud to lead them along the way, and by night in a pillar of fire to give them light, that they might travel by day and by night.* (Exodus 13:21 ESV).

There were no sleeping bags and campfire s'mores. They travelled by day *and night,* and why? So they could get to a sea they couldn't cross! A dead end that trapped them with enemies closing in. It would be impossible without God. That's just the way he wanted it. It's the path he chose if you look at Exodus 13 closely. He didn't want them going back. I began to wonder about my own story. I definitely wanted a sleeping bag to curl up in. I wanted milk and honey. God had other plans, and he didn't want me going back into slavery again.

Then God riveted my attention by another passage that furthered my lesson:

> *Who among you fears the Lord and obeys the word of his servant? Let the one who walks in the dark, who has no light, trust in the name of the Lord and rely on their God* (Isaiah 50:10 NIV).

So – God was teaching me sometimes you walk without resting, and then you run into an obstacle only he can handle. And sometimes you walk where there is no light at all. I thought it was astonishing to find a place in Scripture where the author admits that there might be *no light*. I mean, what happened to "thy word is a lamp unto my feet and a light unto my path? (Psalm 119:105) Well, the Word is illuminating, but it is not the same as a literal light. It helps you navigate the dark, like instruments in an airplane during a storm, or at night. We must navigate by faith when we have no light.

It is here that Isaiah actually warned his hearers the temptation to light torches of their own would result in lying down in torment (Is. 50:11 NIV), and I had certainly lived that. I also know such temptation continues in my life, in big and small ways. I long for the Promised Land partially because I long for an end to all the battles of my life. I want to lie down in green pastures and stay put, God help me!

But even Psalm 23 has been trying to tell me this story: First there is rest, food, and refreshment for the soul, then there is a long walk through the valley of the shadow of death and learning not to fear it, then there are enemies, and finally, there is healing for the wounds of the journey and the gift of a story. Your own story of deliverance! Then, it may start all over again.

We get through the valley by resting when we can, a deep and tested trust, an allowing of God's strength and love to comfort and nourish us as enemies surround. We emerge with new stories of faithfulness. A knowing that *surely* his goodness and mercy is following us.

I could write a whole book about rest and everything God has taught me about the spaces he provides for it even in the midst of chaos. Suffice it to say that when God offers us a place to rest, I think it's a good idea to do so, not worry about whatever else is going on that we can't control. Coronavirus quarantine has provided a great example of this. So many people, stuck at home, unable to change their circumstances by their own power. I want to rest and find gratitude for it. Who but God knows what journey lies ahead? There may be milk and honey involved, but there may also be long journeys through dark valleys, or to seas that we can't cross.

STILL WALKING

God has had quite a project with me. My Mom used to say, "honey, God broke the mold when he made you!" I don't think it was a compliment either – but maybe it's truer than not. I was such a mixed-up mess. All those layers of lies and pretending, hidden beneath spinning and acting as if nothing was wrong. All the colliding emotions of my ambivalence – trust and suspicion, love and hate, need and weakness, longing and self-contempt. Then, on top of everything, I was always in a hurry! Imagine yourself trying to retrain someone like that in clear-headed thinking, patience, and trust (even in the total dark). I don't envy God in the ways he must work to get through our noggins to our hearts. In fact, it's one reason I worship. God is God and I am not.

These new lessons about Promised Land living are making me less naïve and more prepared as I go. They aren't going to make me giddy with joy, but I am more realistic about the mountains that must still be climbed and the seeds that must be buried. And I am more grateful for what I see now as God's provision of milk and honey in the midst of warfare: a place to lay down in peace and rest, a Godly companion on the journey, good friends in the faith and in the fight, and daily bread.

I have learned that I don't only have to fight to win freedom from oppression, I have to fight to keep the freedom I have fought so hard for! Perhaps I have warred and lost, and warred and lost, warred and lost again, but if I am to *not* lose my crown (Revelation 3:11), I must be willing to lose battles and still hold onto faith. I must live more deeply into the truth that the biggest battle of all: The war for peace with God, the war that secured my place in the Kingdom of Heaven – has been won. That was not my battle; but there are battles I must persevere through.

I just have to keep on walking because I am not done yet.

Mine is an unfinished life
With races to run
And pages to write
If I'm walking by faith
And not just by sight
Then mine is an unfinished life

Question: Is there a difference between being disappointed and being discouraged? If so, what? Can you be one without the other?

Question: Where are you in the journey between slavery and being part of a kingdom of priests (representing God to people and people to God) that God imagined? What are your next steps?

Question: How do you walk in the dark with no light (per Isaiah 50:10)? What happens if you get mad at God in the dark and light your own fires (per Isaiah 50:11)?

Action: Just keep walking. In integrity. In humbleness. In prayer. Even in the dark. Just keep walking into the future God saw for you the moment he laid eyes on you.

Author Bio

With a B.A. in Journalism from Texas Tech University and a M.A. from Western Theological Seminary, Amy has spent a lifetime loving words and writing of all kinds. A 20-year career in communications was followed by another 20 years in ministry including worship leading, writing, recovery ministry, and a variety of communications responsibilities. She has written devotional material for *Words of Hope* since 2015, and her current series, *Turning*, will publish in that daily devotional guide in January 2021. Amy serves as ministry associate for a small Vineyard church where she helps with communications and writes a weekday devotional, also found on her blog, https://asipoblog.wordpress.com/. She is married to Fred and they make their home in Michigan. Together, they have five children and five grandchildren that add much joy to life.

Amy is available for speaking, retreats, and guest worship leading. Contact her at walkingwhenyoudratherfly@gmail.com.

To the Reader:

You were my inspiration as this book was outlined several years ago. It became reality in April and May 2020 as our lives became restricted by pandemic. God had been calling me to stay home and write, and now I had no excuse. The book you are holding is the fruit of a 20-year journey, many times painful. But I always told God (as I began to walk back toward him), if the pain could have a purpose, I could stand it. May it be that you are part of that purpose.

Reorders:

At present *Walking When You'd Rather Fly: Meditations on Faith After the Fall* is only available by contacting the author. To order additional copies, please contact the author by email at walkingwhenyoudratherfly@gmail.com.